For Politics:
The Christian, the Church and the State

Published by Ezra Press, a ministry of the Ezra Institute for Contemporary
Christianity, PO Box 9, Stn. Main, Grimsby, ON L3M 1M0

For volume pricing please contact the Ezra Institute:
info@ezrainstitute.ca

For Politics: The Christian, the Church and the State
ISBN: 978-1-989169-15-5

For Politics:
The Christian, the Church and the State

"Christian political action in the scriptural sense...is a battle for a political order that is in conformity with the divine order of creation (sphere-sovereignty), an effort at fundamental and integral reformation or renewal of our political life from out of the Word of God."
– H. Evan Runner

Chapter One:
The Rule of Christ or Cult of the Expert

THE PROBLEM STATED

A sober look at contemporary Western thought in the wake of both the Renaissance and Enlightenment reveals that René Descartes' dictum remains as relevant as ever: "There is nothing so absurd or incredible that it has not been asserted by one philosopher or another." Because ideas have consequences, the ideas of thinkers and philosophers are eventually applied in cultural life. If these are not made subject to the Word of God, they can have disastrous outcomes because they manifest fallen man's rebellion against God's law-order. Today, we live in an era of perpetual revolution manifest by an intense intellectual activism in all cultural and political life. This requires, indeed demands, a distinctly Christian response. But herein lies a serious problem. From where can that Christian response come? What is the basis and *foundation* of a distinctly Christian response to the socio-political crisis of our time? That question is the subject of this monograph.

THE SELF-ANOINTED

Because of the steady triumph of pagan humanism in the West, the modern world has seen the re-emergence of many archaic oddities, one of which is a self-anointed elite class – the *intelligentsia* – a secular substitute for pastor and priest. The first truly modern intellectual, Jean-Jacques Rousseau, set a recognizable tone for the emergence of a self-righteous secular elite, making much of loving an abstraction called "the people," freeing them from the shackles of civilization and tradition, and establishing their "general will." But in the end, he could not disguise his disdain for humanity and likened the masses of ordinary people to "a stupid, pusillanimous invalid."[1]

A more recent defining example of this new class – still celebrated amongst cultural elites today – is George Bernard Shaw, the Irish playwright and public intellectual prominent in the first half of the twentieth century. Beyond writing plays, Shaw held forth on all kinds of cultural and political subjects and made grand sweeping pronouncements about his fellow human beings. Like many British intellectuals of the era, he was a Fabian socialist who nonetheless regarded ordinary working people as contemptible with "no right to live." He wrote, "I should despair if I did not know that they will all die presently, and that there is no need on earth why they should be replaced by people like themselves."[2] Shaw was also an admirer of dictators and political dictatorships precisely because he resented ordinary people influencing culture, believing they could not make sensible decisions. On leaving London for an African vacation in 1935, he remarked, "It is nice to go for a holiday and know that Hitler has settled everything so well in Europe."[3] Though Hitler's antisemitism eventually made it untenable for Shaw to support the national socialism of the Nazis, he remained keen on Stalin and the Soviet dictatorship.[4]

Jean-Paul Sartre, another twentieth-century Western intellectual with a massive cult following – well-known for seducing his young female philosophy students with the help of his lover, Simone de Beauvoir – like Shaw frequently involved himself in cultural and political affairs of which he clearly had no adequate understanding. A man addicted to fornication, alcohol and barbiturates, Sartre proved incapable of maintaining relationships with male intellectual peers who might actually challenge him, and like his radical compatriots, was unable to bring himself to condemn Stalinism or the Communist Party – though he remained gregariously anti-American. He was still publicly defending the Soviets in the 1950s and warmly praising Mao's China. For Sartre, the remnants of an existing Christian political order in the West was simply 'institutionalized violence' that required 'intellectual activism' and 'necessary violence' to overthrow it.[5] In our own time, a majority of Western intellectuals have followed in the wake of thinkers like Sartre and groups like the Frankfurt School, hastening Western culture down into ever deeper levels of depravity, confusion, irrationality and self-immolation.[6] We are forced to ask as Christians, what has gone wrong?

THE FOUNDATION OF WISDOM

It is a regularly observed phenomenon that many otherwise brilliant people appear utterly bereft of wisdom or judgment in the vital affairs of cultural and political life. In response to such imprudence and recklessness, this short work is an effort to articulate a foundation for a distinctly Christian view of politics. In order to do that, and to solve the paradox of cultural and political folly amongst much of the intelligentsia, it is first critical to realize that all cultural and political thought inescapably rests on a given foundation – one religious worldview or another is the frequently unacknowledged basis of all forms of political philosophy. Ultimately, from the scriptural standpoint, either Christ and His Word-revelation provides that foundation, or the thinking of elites and their revolutionary ideals will assume the role of biblical authority. In the older testament, the great Hebrew thinker, politician and teacher, King Solomon, gives us the key to understanding why being intellectually gifted is no guarantee of true insight, wisdom or sound judgment: "The fear of the Lord is the *beginning* of knowledge; fools despise wisdom and discipline ... for the Lord gives wisdom; from His mouth come knowledge and understanding" (Prov. 1:7, 2:6). If the true *foundation* of wisdom is missing, if the *principal part* of knowledge is neglected, then any knowledge structure built upon it is inherently unstable. It may appear elegant and well-proportioned, but when the winds of the real world blow against it, it will be found wanting.

Clearly, intellect, intelligence and wisdom do not always coincide, are certainly not identical, and should never be conflated. A person may have the ability to grasp complex ideas (intellect) and even have the capacity to understand their relevant implications for a given area of thought (intelligence), but *wisdom* is of another character altogether. As Thomas Sowell points out, "wisdom is the rarest quality of all – the ability to combine intellect, knowledge, experience and judgment in a way to produce a coherent understanding. Wisdom is the fulfilment of the ancient admonition, 'With all your getting, get understanding.'"[7]

INTELLECTUALS, REASON AND WORLDVIEW

In the occupational construction of political and cultural ideas, the modern intellectual is usually (there are always exceptions) a person who claims allegiance to a *particular kind* of thinking and a commitment to the use of certain analytical tools and evaluative frameworks. Within these frameworks, ideas that are viewed as progressive or nuanced, novel, enlightened or artistically complex, tend to be applauded whereas 'traditional' ideas are largely dismissed as reactionary, simplistic or outmoded.[8] I remember some years ago a friend who was studying at a Christian university made the traditional assertion that Moses was the author of the first five books of the Bible, to which the instructor replied in a kind of stage whisper "what year is this?" It is perhaps not surprising that few openly and authentically Christian thinkers are welcomed into the exclusive chambers of orthodox intellectual elites.

In contemporary academia, this exclusivity, resting upon a claim of intellectual superiority, presupposes an idea going back to the Enlightenment – that there is an autonomous standard of self-regulating thought (i.e., secular *reasoning)*, protected by an elite class, before which all ideas must present themselves for judgment. Here we encounter the philosophical assumption that human thinking can function as the *lawgiver* of the world, prescribing *from thought* a law to nature. This claim of radical autonomy involving the idea of freedom from anything coming from outside the human subject is the basic idea of Western humanism since the Renaissance. It implies a total rejection of a divinely given *order for* creation. Contemporary trends in this form of thinking that now dominate our culture hold to a *social construction* theory of reality – we can *create* the world we live in by our thought and language, right down to our sexuality and identity. Today we see it expressed throughout the humanities, in economics, politics and law. It is not unusual for intellectuals to then protect these various judgments of their enlightened thought with the claim of *neutrality*, while those who disagree are regarded as uninformed, prejudiced, or hopelessly *biased*.

However, to make this appeal to a supposed *neutrality*, the basis of which is nothing but an established consensus amongst elites, is to assert that our rational behaviour is *self-normed*. This is something the true Christian is obligated to reject because, from a scriptural standpoint, the criteria for rational communication are *given with creation,* and *hold* for all rational pursuits. The criteria for meaningful discourse cannot be *derived* from the participants but must *hold* for them if there are to be universal normative standards for rational behavior. However, such an assertion of universal normative standards for thinking immediately threatens the pretended *autonomy* of the secular intellectual's thought – including his political thought. In other words, the question arises, how can human thinking be a *law unto itself* if it is bound by normative standards given with creation? Both convictions cannot be true at the same time.

To make this point clearer, it is important to recognize that there is a difference between a *norm or law*, and that which is being *subject* to that norm or law. For example, there is a law for the functioning of human cells, but the various individual cells are not identical with the *law for* the cell, neither do they generate that law, because laws are the *conditions which hold* for the existence of something. In a similar way our thinking and discourse (analytical and logical activities) are being *subjected* to norms constantly – in fact political debate presupposes that subjection. The crucial issue becomes: what is the *nature* of those norms? Are they *generated* by the thought of elites (i.e., laws *for* rational thought and thought itself are identical) or are they divinely created, supra-individual normative standards? With this question we are confronted with what the South African philosopher Danie Strauss calls "direction-giving ultimate commitments transcending the realm of rationality itself, since they are embedded in some or other world-and-life-view."[9] This immediately exposes the *non-neutrality* of all thought and shows that replacing revelation with a prevailing *trust* in autonomous 'reason' is not itself rational, but makes its appeal to beliefs and convictions that transcend the rational aspect of life.

Another important observation relevant to this discussion is that logical principles themselves do not provide the *grounds* for believing the *content* of certain arguments to be true or false; they can only help determine if the structure of a given argument is valid i.e., whether or not certain fallacies are present. As Karl Popper once put it, "[Since] all arguments must proceed from assumptions, it is plainly impossible to demand that all assumptions should be based on arguments." Which is simply to say, we already have to *believe* in something to begin to *justify* something else. Christians must always keep in mind that it is not thinking that thinks, but *human beings* – who are much more than their analytical function – that think. All human beings nurture basic beliefs and religious motives that give direction to their thinking, shaping the socio-political vision they advocate, and which inescapably inform the socio-political solutions they offer. As Thomas Sowell points out:

> Intellectuals do not simply have a series of isolated opinions on a variety of subjects. Behind those opinions is usually some coherent *over-arching conception of the world*, a social vision. Intellectuals are like other people in having visions – some intuitive sense of how the world works, what causes what... At the heart of the social vision prevalent among contemporary intellectuals is the belief that there are 'problems' created by existing institutions and that 'solutions' to these problems can be excogitated by intellectuals. This vision is both a vision of society and a vision of the role of intellectuals within society.[10]

The conception of the world dominant in our time has a lineage which stretches back via the Enlightenment to the Renaissance in its revival of pagan Greek thought. For a time, the biblical movement of the Reformation pushed back against this essentially neo-pagan tide by confronting people with the living God and His Word in its central religious significance. But with the protracted religious wars, disillusionment set in regarding the Christian church and so humanism revived and was emboldened by its new alliance with the rise of modern science – despite the development of the sciences being indebted to and dependent upon an essentially biblical view of reality.[11] The subsequent Enlightenment era doubled down on the assumptions of the Renaissance and as a movement had much wider and greater penetration into the various aspects of people's lives. Christian resistance to the spread of unbelief again appeared with the evangelical Great Awakening. As is clear from the journals, letters and writings of the great men of that remarkable revival, though the period saw incredible fruit in evangelism and the development of personal piety, it lacked the rigor and theological depth of the Reformation era and generally missed the cultural scope of *application* for the Word seen amongst the Puritans. It gave preeminent attention to individual salvation of the soul with very little said about the cultural and political life of the nations. The later twentieth century development of Christian Bible colleges and seminaries (and in many cases Christian universities) did not have a root-and-branch reformation in thought and culture in view, but the protection and training of youth for a particular denomination or doctrinal loyalty. H. Evan Runner's analysis is telling:

Failing to confront humanism in any central and comprehensive way, the Evangelical Revival stemmed the revolutionary tide less than the Reformation had done, and in fewer places. The Western world was rapidly becoming post-Christianly pagan. By the middle of the nineteenth century the educated class of Europe had broken overwhelmingly with any Christian point of view. In this way we can understand that humanism has been the dominant cultural driving force or mind in modern Western civilization, which, by taking possession of the hearts of untold millions, and by gaining control of our centres of authority and education, has undergone development and been given expression in and through the successive experiences of western men... Protestants came to withdraw either into a very restricted world of theological argument and investigation or, pietistically, into their private personal lives of 'devotion,' failing to understand that the Word of God was given as light under which man was to live his life by on this earth... In none of the Protestant groups was the central "word" of Christ taking on flesh and blood as it was being *related to the conditions of our creaturely existence* in the continuing experiences of men through the modern centuries.[12]

Few things could be clearer in the early part of the twentieth century than the urgent need for a comprehensive, scripturally rooted development of the *Christian mind*, and the application of this perspective to all of life, including the sphere of the state and political life. The Christian mind must not look at the world as the unbelieving thinker does – as a conundrum to be reduced to manageable basic components and "built anew" by our cognitive efforts. Nor must we regard our inherited institutions as the root of all evil in need of revolutionizing in terms of the euphoric visions of intellectuals. Sin is buried deep in the heart of man himself, not rooted in human institutions that can simply be reimagined by man's autonomous idea to cleanse away evil (Matt. 15:18-20).

With this in view, we will explore why the gospel of Christ must not be regarded or treated as an inspirational 'idea' that offers immediate 'solutions' to various societal 'problems.' Rather, the gospel declares the kingdom and power of God manifest in both the creative and redemptive work of Jesus Christ, which transforms the heart of man, and in so doing makes a *new creature* out of him. The fruit of this transformation is a Spirit-given vision for Christ's kingdom to come and the will of the Father to be done in every aspect of creation. This God-ordained vision calls not for self-anointed *experts*, but for faithful and Spirit-anointed *servants* committed to the law-Word of God for creation and culture and to excellence in each sphere of life for the glory of God.

A BASIC DIFFERENCE BETWEEN CHRISTIAN AND SECULAR POLITICAL THOUGHT

We have already seen that the *foundation* for thinking between the Christian and non-Christian is radically different. One professes *autonomy (self-law)*, the other *theonomy (God's law)* – meaning a total surrender to the law-Word of Christ in creation and Scripture, in whom are hidden all the treasures of wisdom and knowledge (Col. 2:3). This theonomic orientation is lucidly described by Runner:

> God's Law is God's Word. Because God is God, His every Word is Law. From the very first words of the Bible we hear, "And God said, Let there be" this and that. All such creative words are the Law. The Law is what causes creatures and the whole creation to hang together; it determines the conditions of all creaturely existence. It is itself concentrated in the religious law of life: Walk before me according to my commandments and live. Here we have the heart of the creation. The Law determines what it means to live before God, or to die before God.[13]

In the fantasy of autonomy, the modern intellectual, embodying the spirit of our times, essentially pretends to the realization of a new priesthood within society, incarnating a new source of ultimate authority by setting aside *the* prophet, priest and king, Jesus Christ and his kingdom people. Such intellectuals as a class tend to regard themselves as representing a *concentration point* of human knowledge and understanding. As secular bishops, they *mediate* their ideas by influencing and shaping those who will then proclaim and disseminate their vision for them – a kind of substitute clergy in media and education, law, *politics* and arts known as the *intelligentsia*. Only by a deliberate and purposeful act of submission to God's Word-revelation can the Christian thinker avoid the conceits of a godless intelligentsia. This submission to God's Word must in turn lead to the development of a coherent and systematic Christian world-and-life view that serves the kingdom of God by mediating not man's word, but the Word of a comprehensive gospel, to every aspect of human life in all creation.

Second, because of a submission to God and His Word-revelation, not only is the Christian thinker totally subject to Scripture, he or she is also accountable to the normative structure of created reality as God has ordained it by His Law-Word. This means that true Christian thinking is willingly and joyfully submitted to God's Word in creation and does not attempt to remake it after human imagination. Rather than submitting to revelation, from the time of Plato and Aristotle, intellectuals have tended to engage in abstract thought-experiments making playthings of the lives of people in the name of their greater insight or apprehension of 'natural law.' From Plato's *Republic* and Aristotle's *Politics* to Sir Thomas More's *Utopia* and Karl Marx's *Das Kapital*, Western civilization has been profoundly impacted by different styles of social thought-experiment that deal with people, politics and culture in the *abstract* – as these thinkers would *prefer* persons and the world to be – but which do not really grapple with the world and history in its *givenness*. Outside of the laboratory of the mind, however, such thought-experiments have real-life consequences. The atheistic materialism of Marx's thought, with its abstract revolutionary masses throwing off the evils of wage labor and private property, supposedly leading mankind toward total freedom in a stateless and work-free world, has cost millions of people their lives. During the age of the Enlightenment *philosophes*, Rousseau attacked Christian civilisation and idealized the 'noble savage' whilst abandoning all of his own children to a hospice where they almost certainly died. In more recent decades John Rawls described a 'veil of ignorance' in contractarian political theories of society, positing imaginary worlds free from metaphysical beliefs or cultural history. All such abstractions are erroneous in large measure because they are inattentive to the human condition and social reality.

One of the important differences between the occupation of intellectuals and that of the engineer is that engineers find themselves constantly *accountable to the real world* if they make mistakes. If I make a mistake with a historical or philosophical reference in one of my articles or lectures, I may get a kind (or angry) email from a reader pointing out my error, but if my brother Daniel who is a heating engineer (designing and installing complex heating systems in commercial properties) makes a serious mistake, real college dorm rooms or somebody's office will be flooded, or catch fire, or explode. There is an immediate accountability here in the concrete world of experience – an external standard of accountability. An engineer whose designs and work prove to be a repeated failure will not long be in the industry. Yet if an intellectual has a grand new idea, happens to be or become influential and the idea is applied but fails, that thinker is often seen as a brave pioneer or prophet out of time. At other times, as so clearly manifest in Marxist social theory, the blame for the failure of the thinker's ideas is placed on 'society' or others' 'faulty interpretation or application,' and not infrequently on the stupidity of the masses for the philosophy not working.

Take current gender theories like those of Judith Butler which assert that sex is 'fictive' i.e., a creation of *political language regimes* forming perceptions of the body as having male and female identity, but which are in fact just forms of oppression. Or consider feminist theories seeking to level all distinctions between men and women, and various other forms of deconstructionist critical theory. External tests in the real world that would be applied to the engineer don't seem to apply here. The only test that seems to matter is what other feminists, queer theorists and critical theorists amongst the intelligentsia think; do they find the ideas original, appropriately subversive of authority, or progressive and imaginative? When the lives, education and socio-economic future of children, families and society are destroyed by the application of these intellectuals' near-unintelligible word games, the blame is placed on societal taboos, the patriarchal family, traditional institutions, structural inequality and systemic racism for things not working out well. The givenness of creation and God's law-word for society, which is what invariably frustrates their purpose, is dismissed as simply a power-structure to be revolted against.

Consider again the various shades of Marxist political philosophy that have been tried numerous times on various continents with the same devastating and tragic results; the repeated failure doesn't stop intellectuals committed to an abstract ideology continuing to venerate Marxist social theory whilst blaming a faulty application or nuance of interpretation for the economic devastation or vicious death of multitudes. This is because their criteria for judgment is essentially *internal,* not *external* – which is to say man must *prescribe,* not discover and *acknowledge,* the normative structures for human life. Thus, in the name of intellectual freedom, unaccountability becomes a hallmark of the occupation of both the intellectual and the intelligentsia which follows them. The noted British intellectual, John Stuart Mill, went as far as to argue that intellectuals should be free even from social standards, all the while setting those standards for others.[14] It is existing institutions and traditions, norms and standards that must change to accommodate the intellectuals' ideas, not the thinker who must be subject to laws and norms in the created world.

In marked contrast, the Christian must submit their thinking to Scripture and explore the various spheres of the creation order as *revelation* from God. Together, these have a 'norming' impact on Christian thought, giving concrete direction to the believer's labors in every sphere – including the political. The thought-products of Christians can then be judged by and made accountable to an external standard, just as the prophets in Scripture were judged in terms of their faithfulness to the Word of God and accuracy of their description of God's historical activities.

THE CULT OF THE EXPERT OR THE WORSHIP OF CHRIST

One of the besetting sins of professional intellectuals as a class is believing that, because they have a particular depth of knowledge or strong ability in a given area, they can then generalize their narrow knowledge and ability into the notion of their own superior wisdom and judgement for life in general. Frequently disregarding the everyday, non-theoretical and mundane knowledge of ordinary people in the real world, central socio-political planning is taken on by the 'experts' – a particular kind of intellectual – as part of a broader intelligentsia who believe they alone are qualified to guide and shape society. As Thomas Sowell has rightly pointed out, "Intellectuals have seen themselves not simply as an elite – in the passive sense in which large landowners, rentiers, or holders of various sinecures might qualify as elites – but as an *anointed* elite, people with a mission to lead others in one way or another toward better lives."[15]

We have seen this modern cult at work during the era of the Covid-19 related crisis, with intellectuals in the fields of virology, statistics and computer modelling wheeled out by politicians to proclaim that civil liberties should be suspended for months on end, while prophesying that life can never return to the way it was before if we are to have a safe and healthy future. Because they are the 'experts', few pause to ask what qualifies a virologist, computer modeller or statistician to make far-reaching social, political and juridical decisions that profoundly affect millions of people around the world, including those of us in ostensibly free societies. But according to the politicians we must all be guided by the 'experts'.

Another good example is seen in the field of economics – a bamboozling subject for the uninitiated as literal 'magic tricks' are performed by financial experts. For most of us ordinary mortals, we assume that paper money must *represent* a specific value of something concrete that has a generally agreed worth. Therefore, a certain number of dollars will buy me a certain number of potatoes (the paper being monetized wealth for the purpose of trade). Countries in which trust in their currency evaporates – as was seen in Zimbabwe, the former Soviet Union and is taking place now in Venezuela – soon find that a wheelbarrow full of paper money will not buy them a loaf of bread because their money is suspected of being no longer backed by something real and reliable; inflation having pushed the price of goods that much higher. Yet we are told by experts today that modern economies do not need to be backed by gold and other precious metals but can function safely simply on debt and government promises. The political answer to financial crises is therefore not 'austerity' and a balanced budget, but more and more public spending and *stimulus* to grow the economy. Stimulus means quantitative easing (that is, printing more and more paper money), with governments accumulating more and more debt, supported by the promise of future tax revenues and economic growth (GDP). As money gets cheaper due to its increased availability, keeping interest rates artificially low, many people borrow more, whilst the savings of others are effectively devalued (money now being worth less). However, markets inevitably aware of the problem will be concerned with looming runaway inflation. The sustainability of this model is therefore predicated on the ideas of unending economic growth and trust in government experts manipulating economic reality. Thus, for most Western governments, the idea of a balanced budget has gone the way of the dodo.

Whatever we make of this, the point is that economic and monetary policy is not value-neutral but equally driven by the thinking of expert-intellectuals who are not simply accountants and economists but people shaping life and culture in terms of a *worldview*, believing they are uniquely qualified to guide society. As Stephen D. King notes:

> The idea that monetary policy is politically neutral is a convenient fiction rather than a reflection of reality. Yet it is often only during periods of economic and social upheaval that the fiction is exposed. Today, monetary policy works not so much by reinvigorating the economy but, instead, by redistributing wealth and income: it is no more than a stealthy form of redistributive taxation.[16]

There is nothing truly new here. Whether the area is economic life, law, medicine, education, politics or some other area of cultural import, from the time of the Pharaoh's magicians and the Persian magi, kings, emperors and political leaders have surrounded themselves with a cadre of 'experts' to both give counsel and to act as a convenient means of shifting blame if things went wrong. Of course the intellectuals of the ancient and classical world did not enjoy the same levels of unaccountability that the modern expert enjoys. If you misinterpreted Pharaoh's dream or that of the king of Babylon, you might be executed. But whether they were called satraps or soothsayers, advisers or counselors, scholars or magi, they were the public intellectuals of their era and frequently functioned as a priestly class guiding the religious and political life of the people. These thinkers, however, were invariably fumbling in the darkness, disconnected from the revealed covenants of promise and often oblivious to the clarity of God's revelation in creation. Unless any expert intellectual is willingly subject to Christ and His Word-revelation, even when they stumble across God's creational laws and norms in their work, they will consistently fail to properly apply what they have learned in terms of the fullness of the wisdom of God – for as we have seen, intellect, intelligence and wisdom are not same thing.

PROPHETIC THINKING IN POLITICS

Nonetheless, from a scriptural standpoint, there remains an important role for the person whose work-product is ideas – there is a legitimate task for the intellectual in cultural and political life. In the Bible we notice it is God who gives his servant Joseph *wisdom* in pagan Egypt to understand the times, advise and serve in political office and correctly interpret dreams given by God to Pharaoh for the deliverance of both Egypt and Joseph's family from famine (Acts 7: 9-16). Along with the famed king Solomon, who gave us the books of Ecclesiastes, Proverbs and Song of Solomon, and whose careful observations and wise applications of God's Law-Word in creation and Scripture brought even the queen of Sheba to hear him (1 Kings 10:1-9), perhaps the best example of a believing political thinker and public intellectual in Scripture is that of Daniel. Because of his lineage and gifts, he is specifically recruited into an elite school for the ancient equivalent of experts or intellectuals: scholars and thinkers among whom some would give guidance to society and government (Dan. 1:3-6). Along with some noble friends from Judah (Shadrach, Meshach and Abednego), noted for their resistance to idolatry to the point of being cast into a fiery furnace, Daniel is identified as having real potential as an advisor in the king's court for the government of the people.

These men determined to honor God in their occupation from the start. As a result, the Bible tells us, "God gave these four young men knowledge and understanding in every kind of literature and wisdom. Daniel also understood visions and dreams of every kind ... no one was found equal to Daniel... so they began to serve in the king's court. In every matter of wisdom and understanding that the king consulted them about, he found them 10 times better than all the diviner-priests and mediums in his entire kingdom" (Dan. 1:17-21). Daniel and his friends went on to distinguish themselves, finding high position in the realm and government of Babylon, where in God's providence they exercised profound influence for the *kingdom of God* from the head of state down. This was possible because they were granted knowledge, wisdom and understanding by the Lord Himself and determined to obey God's commands and serve diligently to His glory.

These men were intimately acquainted with the truth that the *fear of the Lord is the beginning of wisdom.* The other intellectuals and government advisors lacked such understanding and prophetic perception because the foundation of their thought was wanting. They lacked insight into the normative structure of creation because they were unsubmitted to the Law-Word of God. The advantage that Daniel and his friends enjoyed should be even more apparent with the Christian thinker who is self-consciously subject to God's Word in Scripture and creation. In Christ all the treasures of wisdom and knowledge are hid (Col. 2:3), meaning that the Christian thinker can avoid the pitfalls and mistakes of a godless intelligentsia by apprehending and appreciating all things in their true context, from within a scriptural world-and-life view. This makes the Christian mind unique, containing a prophetic power that comprehends all creation as an instantiation of the Word of God.

In the final analysis, as valuable as the insights of all those who make careful study of any of the marvelous functions of creation can be, our trust and hope will either be in Christ and His Word-revelation or the expertise of autonomous man. The history of every era is littered with the false prophecy of the intelligentsia of that time. To place ultimate trust in the 'ideas' of people is a fool's gambit, like the unwise man who built his house upon the sands of lawlessness. But to put our trust in Christ and His Law-Word is to be wise and build our house on the rock (Matt. 7:21-27). Men's ideas come and go, but the Word of the Lord stands forever. The gospel of the kingdom is not man's tyrannous political idea, but the redemptive and restorative Word of God for every area of life. Only in this Word is there life and freedom for human society. In the memorable words of the historian Paul Johnson, "we must at all times remember what intellectuals habitually forget...the worst of all despotisms is the heartless tyranny of ideas."[17]

Contrary to popular opinion, Scripture does give Christians a mandate to apply the wisdom of God's law-Word to political life rather than relying on the ideas of godless people. To neglect this task is to faithlessly abandon our society and culture to despotism and tyranny.

Chapter Two:
The Church, the State and the Kingdom of God

THE PRACTICAL REALITY

Having considered the basic antithesis between the Lordship of Christ and His Word and the rule of autonomous man and his ideas within society, we are immediately confronted with the practical question of the Christian's calling in regard to politics. This is especially acute with respect to the life of the church institute and its relationship to the rest of culture. It is not uncommon for confusion and suspicion to quickly arise among Christians when anyone suggests that Christ's Lordship has concrete implications for political life. Does this imply the hammer of a clergy-governed theocracy coming down upon a nation? More broadly and often struggling to frame the questions properly, modern Western Christians frequently wrestle with whether the church should involve itself in political matters or regard itself as an essentially private 'spiritual' realm that does not occupy its time with 'secular' issues? In short, if God's people are to be involved in politics in some way, what is this meant to look like? These are thorny problems that have become increasingly important for Christians to grapple with as Western culture has continued apace to repaganize.

A FALSE DILEMMA

For the most part, believers tend to think that they are confronted with a very restricted choice in these matters: either pursue a return to a form of the ecclesiastical culture of Christendom where power and authority over various cultural and political matters is restored to a particular church denomination, or accept that we now live in a post-Christian age where the only thing Christians can realistically hope for is being one of many interest groups in a diverse, multicultural society, with perhaps a seat at the table – a chair pulled out for us by a humanistic secular state now to be embraced as the norm for human society.

Of these limiting alternatives, the second view presently dominates modern evangelicalism. It has therefore become popular in Christian circles to follow the culture in bashing the Roman Emperor Constantine as a bogeyman – the founder of a wholly bad Christendom model in Western history. It is also a way to score easy points in academic circles, since it conforms to the orthodox conventions of critical theory in the universities. As a consequence, any Christian who desires and works to see a strong influence for the Christian faith shaping cultural and political life risks being accused of being "Constantinian" – and is therefore also regarded as a potentially dangerous theocrat, ominously lurking in the wings of history for an opportunity to destroy people's liberties and oppress them. Such a perspective is not only ignorant but a base ingratitude for the incalculable blessings that came to the Western world through the ecclesiastical culture of Christendom, not merely in terms of visible architecture for tourists, but the development of a free university, freedom of the church, canon law and Christian law codes, hospitals, a rich and astonishing legacy of music and art and much more besides. There is certainly a great deal for the believer to be thankful for in looking back on the Christianizing of the ancient emperor in Byzantium – most notably the cessation of a terrible and protracted persecution of Christians.

A tragically common response to pointing out such benefits is the glib romanticizing of political persecution as an ideal state for the church by Western believers who have never experienced it – which is, to put it mildly, naïve. Worse, to pretend to wish for such a situation in the name of spiritual health or growth for the church in our time is the epitome of zeal without knowledge and not knowing what spirit we are of (Prov. 19:2; Luke 9:55-56). The apostles urged the church to pray for political leaders and all those in high positions so that Christians would be left in peace to live quiet, godly lives. They did not intercede for state-sanctioned persecution for the sake of church growth or rooting out nominalism in Christian congregations (1 Tim. 2:1-2). In fact, Paul used his political rights as a Roman citizen to escape flogging and persecution and legally appealed his own case all the way to Caesar to avoid execution by the Jews (Acts 22:25ff; Acts 25:1-27). While they endured courageously, the early church clearly did not view persecution as an ideal state for believers, and the fourth century Christians would have regarded the conversion of the emperor Constantine as a mighty work of God's deliverance – which it most certainly was!

That being said, it must also be readily recognized that the transition from a state of political persecution in the early centuries to what relatively quickly became one of power and wealth for the heads of some of the churches under Constantine and many of his successors brought with it a great many temptations which became the occasion for gradual internal decay within the church – just as the temptation to compromise with progressive culture for the easy life in North America is a cause of internal decay in modern evangelicalism. Moreover, though leaving *internal church affairs* to the bishops, Constantine believed he was appointed by God as the *bishop for external affairs.* And, while he did many good things, like the revolutionary ending of a bloodthirsty death cult in the frenzied arenas of the Roman Empire, the long-term results of his conflation of church authority and civil governmental power were very mixed, both in the East and West. He unquestionably set the stage for a historical conflict between church and state. Right up to this day, the Orthodox church is built on governmental authority, and prior to the Russian Revolution, the Czar had the same power in the Russian church as Constantine had claimed for himself.

The result of this early misunderstanding of the church's proper function produces difficulties in discerning the jurisdiction and calling of the Christian church in relation to the rest of society (especially the state) that have revealed themselves again and again. For example, Sean Field, history professor at the University of Vermont in an article on the rise of royal power in France, noted that by the end of the Capetian period in 1328, "France…was imagined as a 'new holy land' and the French as a 'new chosen people,' with the royal family appointed to defend the kingdom on God's behalf."[18]

France was not the only European power in the Late Middle Ages and beyond with the habit of inappropriately conflating the church institute, the state, and the kingdom of God. Especially in the decades immediately prior to the Reformation, there was a profound lack of clarity among Christians surrounding the character, task and jurisdiction of the church as it relates to God's kingdom in the earth – and much confusion persisted even after the Reformation. In our cultural moment, a profound fog of confusion has descended and thickened among Western evangelicals around the same issue, with significant consequences resulting for God's people as society continues to de-Christianize at an alarming rate.

To address this problem, the first task will be to consider the *nature* of the church in its relationship to other social entities and societal institutions – with a particular focus on the state. This will of necessity involve exploring the church's relation to the biblical conception of the kingdom of God. I hope to show that choosing between a revival of the ecclesiastical culture of Christendom or the acceptance of a radically relativized place for Christianity and the church in a normalized secular culture is a *false dilemma*. Which is to say, these are not the only ways of thinking about the church and the role and responsibility of Christians in relation to political life. The journey will involve untangling some theological and philosophical knots and escaping a historical maze of confusion regarding the church and her important relation to other God-ordained spheres of life.

CONFUSING THE ROLE OF CHURCH AND STATE

As hinted already, the challenge of properly situating the church's relationship to the rest of human society and the broader concept of the kingdom of God is best illustrated by exploring the longstanding struggle between the church and state. In fact, it is the very best place to start because this issue has been critically important in shaping ideas about the nature of the church, the character of national cultures, and the regulation of socio-political life in the West.

At the outset, it must be readily acknowledged that the institutional church has frequently claimed a role for itself in politics that goes well beyond what Scripture teaches about the life and function of the *instituted church* within a social order. Abraham Kuyper observed:

> While we…may not place church and state over against each other as two heterogeneous powers, history shows how very difficult it is to define the correct relationship between the two. Both of them are to blame for this. It is certainly not only the heroes of the state that restricted the rightful position of the church; there were just as many attempts on the part of the church to *extend its power beyond legitimate boundaries.*

The old battle between pope and emperor continued after the reformation, albeit in a different form.[19]

During the history of Christendom, ecclesiastical authorities often sought to accrue to the church institute powers and jurisdiction properly belonging to the state (and other spheres of life), thereby creating a kind of societal ecclesiocracy. However, the emergence of this state of affairs is completely understandable when viewed in historical and theological context. The early church, rooted in the scriptures, understood that the gospel had in view a *worldwide kingdom* and empire of Jesus Christ; the kingdoms of the earth were becoming the kingdoms of our Lord and of His Christ (Rev. 11:15). Moreover, in the present age, Jesus Christ is ruler of the kings of the earth (Ps. 2; Rev. 1:5). The preaching of this gospel of the kingdom was clearly for all peoples under heaven and the nations were to be taught and discipled in obedience to everything Christ commanded (Matt. 28:16-20). Moreover, in the context of this worldwide kingdom the church as Christ's spiritual body and called-out people was ultimately one and catholic – which simply means *universal.*

There was nothing wrong with this scriptural understanding of the extent of the dominion and empire of Jesus Christ (cf. Ps. 2; 110; Is. 42:1-9; Rev. 1:5); the problems emerge in understanding how this dominion expresses itself in the various societal institutions. As the Roman Empire broke into Eastern and Western parts, leading to the division of a Greek Orthodox and Western church, over time imperial Rome emerged in the foreground, dominated by a relatively undifferentiated hierarchical power structure in which church and state had become entwined in one another. As the Roman empire began to fail, power shifts resulted. Kuyper's description of the result is telling:

> When the *imperial* power of Rome faded, then the *ecclesiastical* influence of the bishop of Rome increased. It was inevitable that the ecclesiastical power, which continued to develop under this hierarchical presidency of the pope, became the competitor to the decaying political unity...the Roman Empire...gradually crumbled altogether.... And since the significance of the political unity of power continually diminished, it was inevitable that the ecclesiastical power – which even more strongly possessed a universal character – eventually overshadowed the political power. This could change only when the Roman Empire was transferred to the Germanic nations as the "Holy Roman Empire," but this happened by making an ever-stronger opposition between emperor and pope. The doctrine of the two swords entered the world...; the pope was to be honored as the representative of Christ, and therefore all worldly power should be subject to Rome's tribunal.[20]

This meant that in much of Europe the word of the pope became effective law.

This view of the church itself as a universally instituted power over all life was reinforced in the High and Late Middle Ages because Roman Catholic theology, as mediated through the Aristotelianism of Thomas Aquinas, regarded the church as belonging to a domain of *grace*, above and superior to *nature*.[21] This involved a strictly hierarchical view of reality and society with the church perched at the top as the gateway to eternal perfection and bliss – the state playing a support role in bringing people toward earthly moral perfection. The church's 'super-natural' theology of grace, a *donum supperadditum* (an added gift), meant that for culture to be *Christian* it had to be an *ecclesiastical culture* – that is, largely led and governed by the instituted church – upheld by the authority and ecclesiastical sanction of the pope over kings and commoners. In other words, the various spheres of life needed to be *churchified* and brought within the wide embrace of ecclesiastical authority if they were to be purified and have lasting value – especially politics. Church involvement or oversight was seen as sanctifying otherwise profane activities and spheres of life.

The church hierarchy of the Middles Ages thus became entrenched in a protracted struggle with numerous princes and emperors to control the affairs of various realms and kingdoms, sometimes even employing the power of the sword to accomplish its ends – a power that God had clearly given to the state (cf. Rom. 13:1-4), not to the institutional church. For as long as this supposedly *sacred realm* of the church (an upper storey of *grace*) held sway over a secular realm of *nature* (a lower storey of reality including the *political institution of the state*), a semblance of Christian society could be maintained in the form of a unified ecclesiastical culture. But with the Renaissance toward the end of the Middle Ages, the overarching authority of the church institution was steadily undermined and the tenuous union of *nature* (reason, family, state, education, arts etc.,) and *grace* (the church with her ecclesiastical authority and theology) was shattered. The so-called realm of 'nature' no longer wanted the 'super-natural' to rule over or supervise it and the West began *secularizing.*

Along with the Renaissance came the steady rise of universities and a revival of pagan Greek thought. A concurrent spiritual decay was taking place in the church where the gospel was being increasingly obscured – both realities meant a growing resistance to an ecclesiastical domination of life. As a consequence, the church of Rome's authority steadily weakened. People began to feel that the relationship of church and state was distorted by the assertion that civil authority was *derived* in part from the bishop of Rome. The desire for renewal and reformation in church and society culminated in the sixteenth century Reformation, which split the Western church in two. "The papist power lost its universal significance and the church, after the attempt to lord it over the state, now in turn became subject to the power of the state."[22]

The *subjection* of the church to the state proved just as problematic for the church and society in general as the subjection of the state to the church had done. Despite the Reformation, which broke emphatically with Rome, different protestant churches sought to have themselves established as the *official church* of a given state or realm. This arrangement where the state assumes an effective leadership over the church is called *caesaropapism.*

It is well understood that under Martin Luther's leadership, since the churches in Germany needed the support of German princes to break the hierarchical power of Rome, the tendency was to *subject the church* more extensively to the state. In Lutheran domains the princes were given power not just *over* the church, but claimed a spiritual influence *within* it, receiving episcopal rank to function as leaders with Luther's agreement. The same is true in many Eastern European countries with an established state church. The Church of England established by Henry VIII also effectively broke with Rome. Here the regal head of state became the head of the church. A little later in the seventeenth century, even the evangelical Scots, negotiating with the English Parliament in conflict with Charles I, sought to have Presbyterianism established as the official state church in England and failed – in part because many of the puritans in the Cromwellian era favoured the independence of the churches. However, with the return of Charles II in 1660, a series of Acts was eventually passed called the Clarendon Code which persecuted protestants who were not part of the Church of England.

Despite all this, with the Calvinistic branch of the Reformation, a different view of the church's relationship to the state did begin to emerge – a theme we will return to in more detail later. It is true that these reformed protestant churches initially needed the military might of their rulers to resist Spain, Austria and France to prevent the destruction of Protestantism in its infancy, but the theological resources to reject the Roman view (that saw the church institute as over civil government) and the Lutheran view (that saw the state ruling over the church) were present and ready to be developed where a truly independent church influenced political life by means other than government establishment, subsidy or control. The Westminster Confession of 1647 lays out the general contours of this position: "The Lord Jesus, as King and Head of His Church, hath therein appointed a government in the hand of Church officers distinct from the civil magistrate" (chapter 30, section 1). As Greg Bahnsen points out in his detailed analysis of the Confession:

> [T]he Confession guards the separation of church and state by keeping the civil magistrate out of ecclesiastical business and jurisdiction. Moreover, the Confession protects the state from authoritative intervention or intrusive jurisdiction by the church ... The magistrate may appeal to the church for advice, or in extraordinary cases the church may out of conscience rebuke the actions of the magistrate; but the church is prohibited from meddling, handling or concluding matters which pertain solely to civil affairs. It should be noted that certain matters of public morality are not solely the concern of the commonwealth.[23]

Ever since the Enlightenment, secularization has not meant maintaining a jurisdictional separation of church and state – which was already maintained by the reformed confessions; contemporary secularization constitutes an effort to jettison altogether both the church *institute* and God Himself from all aspects of so-called 'nature' (i.e., most of everyday life, culture and politics) in order to maximize space for the 'free play' of the human personality. This has pushed the old unified ecclesiastical vision of Roman Catholicism further and further back into its own microcosm where the conflation of church and state remains most overt. In Vatican City – an independent city state enclaved within Rome (the smallest sovereign state in the world) – the state is ruled by an absolute elective monarch, the pope. Though a distinct entity, Vatican City is under the dominion and sovereign authority of the *Holy See*. The Vatican's legal system is distinct from that of Italy and the Bishop of Rome is head of state and church, exercising ex-officio supreme legislative, executive, and judicial power.

As already noted, however, the fault in problematic church/state relations has not solely resided with the church. Historically *the state* has regularly sought to usurp the authority and role of the church. We have seen that with *caesaropapism* in both east and west, it was often civil governments and states that for political purposes wanted the official establishment of particular churches so that they could be controlled, manipulated, or put to political purpose. Because of the established Church in England, even today, the British Prime Minister is required to play an important role in the selection of the Archbishop of Canterbury which, since they are political appointees, has significant implications for the English church. Due in part to their positions of political power and state support, compromised or faithless bishops often play the role of chaplains to the secular state in the House of Lords, rubber-stamping the progressive drift rather than standing faithfully for the truth of the gospel. The British monarch is also Head of the Church of England and *Defensor fidei* (defender of the faith), but this has meant little or nothing in recent decades to arrest decline and decay in the establishment.

Despite its many faults, at least in this system the Church of England has been historically regarded as something important and unique in society, functioning in the past as a conscience for the nation and could expect a certain amount of respect, protection and recognition from civil government. However, in the Erastian collegial system which obtains in places like the Netherlands, there is no material difference between a church, a mosque, a Buddhist temple, a synagogue, or a sports club. They are simply regarded by the state as various 'societies' which government must ensure will respect civil law and not hinder individual freedom. There is no recognition in civil government that God is at work in a special way in the life and witness of Christian churches, nor do they enjoy a unique independence that would distinguish them from a soccer club or a society of Jedi knights. Churches have gradually become 'societies' to be controlled and managed by the 'neutral' state. Abraham Kuyper opined:

> Caesaropapism assumes power over the church, and then the church turns to stone. If the modern state denies the autonomous character and higher right of Christ's church, then the church degenerates into the status of a society or an entirely ordinary association.[24]

At the more extreme end of state interference and control, in various dictatorships of the modern era the church has been grossly assaulted, used and manipulated. In Nazi Germany for example, Hitler sought to seize control of the national church and use it to further his own messianic claims. The German

Evangelical Church in the grip of caesaropapism had a long and misguided tradition of subservient loyalty to the state. In the 1920s, a movement emerged within this church called the "German Christians" (*Deutsche Christen*). Under the influence of the Nazi state in the 1930s, these people embraced many aspects of Nazi thinking and sought the creation of a national "Reich Church" which promoted a nazified version of Christianity. In opposition to the "German Christians" a "Confessing Church" (*Bekennende Kirche*) emerged. Their *Barmen Declaration* asserted that the church's allegiance was to God and Scripture and not to any earthly *Führer*. The German Evangelical church was thus divided and a struggle within German Protestantism ensued. Many of the Confessing Church leaders were persecuted, betrayed, imprisoned or executed.

Historian Frank Dikotter notes the religiously tinged claims of various twentieth century dictators:

> Hitler presented himself as a messiah united with the masses in a mystical, quasi-religious bond. Mussolini encouraged feelings of devotion and worship characteristic of Christian piety. There were holy sites, holy pictures, pilgrimages, the hope of a healing touch from the leader. In the Soviet Union, even as the Orthodox Church came under siege, a new religion under the red star appeared, with a corner dedicated to Lenin in factories, offices, restaurants, some of them real altars decorated with ribbons and wreaths. [25]

Conflict, confusion and usurpation as well as manipulation, impersonation and control have thus been commonplace in the history of the West in the relation of church and state – each seeking supremacy over the other at different times and in various circumstances. As Christian faith has declined in influence, Western society has sought to renegotiate its relationship to the church (secularization) and reinterpret its remarkable and enduring Christian history, largely by condemning its own past. At the same time, believers have been left wondering how to understand the role of the church in the current socio-political environment.

WHAT IS THE CHURCH?

To begin to resolve the church-state-society problem, a close look at the nature of the church is required. In view of the fact that religion is basic to all of life (whether Christian, Islamic, pagan, humanistic etc.,) and the inescapable condition of faith within human existence touches all the areas of our experience in the world, many Christians *intuitively* recognize that Christianity must be a faith *for all of life*. That is, they recognize that Christ's claims about Himself, His kingdom and people must be deeply significant beyond their own personal devotion since they appear all- encompassing and universal. However, difficulties arise in considering the *way* these claims *apply* to His *called-out people, the church, in their societal relationships*.

It is these questions surrounding the concrete *application* of Christ's claims which occasion confusion as to the character and calling of the church and how it should relate to the state and other social entities and institutions. For example, should the *church institute* assert itself and its beliefs over other social entities and institutions as the primary agent of the kingdom, or are the kingdom of God and the church institute basically identical so that Christ's sovereign reign need only be manifest in the life of the gathered church congregation? Alternatively, is the reality of Christ's kingdom to shape all of life and culture with the church institute as one of many expressions of that reality? To address this, we need to begin by briefly asking ourselves what the church *is*, and what the church is meant to *do*. This will allow us to consider the relationship of the church and the kingdom of God, and then to define an ideal relationship of the church institute to the state and other societal institutions.

In the scriptures, Christ promises to *build His church* (Matt. 16:18). The Greek term for church is *ekklesia* and is rendered from the Hebrew *Qahal* and *Edah,* which were used as the standing names for the congregation of Israel. The church is therefore a called out and gathered people united into one community by the preaching of the gospel. This people, both Jew and Gentile (Eph. 2), are those that recognize Jesus as Lord, king and messiah and inherit the promises forfeited by the old faithless congregation of Israel. Among this new people are manifest the powers of the world to come. Willem Ouweneel correctly identifies five different senses or meanings of the Christian church found in the New Testament. First, we observe a worldwide, transcendent, *invisible church* which is the *body of Christ*, transcending any temporal period, from its origin to the second coming (Eph. 3:9-11; 5:23-24, 32). Second, we can identify a worldwide, *immanent-historical church* (Eph. 2:21; Col. 2:19), which is the *visible church* here on earth that through development and growth, ruin and renewal traverses a certain history. It comprises all true believers, spread over the whole earth, in all times and places. Third, we have the *worldwide concretely actual church* – the totality of believers at this given moment who are here on earth (Gal. 1:13). Then we can also speak of the *local church*, which is the totality of believers in a city, town or village (Acts 8:1; 13:1; 15:4; Rom. 16:1; Rev. 2-3). In this sense the Greek *ekklesia* can also be used in the plural (1 Cor. 16:1; 2 Cor. 8:1; Rev. 1:4) and can refer to the *meeting* of the local churches (1 Cor. 11:18; Eph. 3:21; Col. 4:16). Finally, we can speak of the *church as a part of the local church* that may meet in various places like the home (Acts 5:14; 12:12; Rom. 16:3-5).[26]

In much modern usage, the worldwide, transcendent element of the invisible body is typically overlooked. People tend to speak of the church as a *building* or as having a regional meaning like the Church of England or the Evangelical (Lutheran) Church of Germany. We tend not to think as much as we should in the broader terms of Scripture's view of the church. In addition, many denominations have arisen in the course of history which consist of various geographically *local congregations* – more or less formally organized within a given hierarchy or administration. So, when people speak of the *Church of England* for example, or the *Fellowship of Evangelical Baptists in Ontario*, we encounter a different meaning of "church" to any of the five mentioned in the Bible. This historical development is not itself wrong, but is important to note because, when we speak of "the church" teaching, evangelizing, engaging the community or doing various other things, we do not mean the invisible universal body of Christ, or the immanent-historical visible church as a whole, but rather this or that locally instituted congregation or denomination. Moreover, in a strict sense, "the church" doesn't teach or evangelize or discipline; different teachers and leaders within local congregations or denominations teach and evangelize, with elders and pastors who discipline.

So, what authority and jurisdiction does the local church institute have apart from singing, praying, preaching and prophesying, evangelizing, disciplining members and celebrating the Lord's Supper? Ouweneel points out:

> [T]his authority applies at most to itself, its own members, and this through its elders. There is no such thing in the Bible as "the" church exercising authority over other societal relationships, over families, over society, even over the state…; this is pure scholasticism, a certain protestant denomination now usurping the position that the Roman Catholic Church had during the Middle Ages…. As an immanent community of people, an association with rulers and regulations, church councils and church fees, every church denomination is, from a purely *structural* point of view, a societal relationship like any other.[27]

It would make no sense to suggest, for example, that the *universal church* has authority over certain areas of a Christian's life – how could that ever be applied meaningfully? It is only local elders who have a limited authority over the believer in the life of the local church.

Why is this important and does this evaluation somehow undermine the importance of the Christian church and its authority? Firstly, there is nothing in this analysis that minimizes the critical importance and significance of the gathered congregation of believers in local churches for worship, prayer, preaching, the sacraments, and the privilege of church discipline. What it shows, however, is that we cannot transfer the significance, jurisdiction or authority of Christ's universal-transcendent body and kingdom reign to the life of any local and historically realized congregation or denomination. Nor can we turn any instituted expression of the church of Christ into "the" church that is now exercising this or that power and authority *over* other spheres of life. It is Christ alone who exercises power and authority through believers *in all spheres* of life. As Ouweneel shows:

> In living my Christian life, my marriage, my family, my local congregation, and even my Christian schools and associations, are equally important as autonomous expressions of the one kingdom of God. In each of these societal relationships, I am under the Lordship of Christ. As such my membership of the local congregation is not more important than my being a Christian husband, parent, professor, businessman, and party member...; the kingdom of God on earth encompasses all these societal associations.[28]

If this were not so, one's relationship to the local church congregation would be elevated over all other supposedly "common institutions," (like marriage, family or vocation) just as "grace" is supposedly elevated over "nature" in all expressions of scholastic philosophy and theology. To be clear, what is *not* being said here is that being a businessman or husband will last forever. The local Christian school my children attend is not an everlasting reality like being a member of the invisible, transcendent body of Christ. However, my local church or even denomination is constantly changing in various ways and will not last forever either. Locally instituted churches are not permanent – just consider the warnings historically fulfilled against the churches in the book of Revelation.

With what can be a startling realization that the role of the church is relativized in its place in terms of the kingdom of God, it is sometimes objected that the scriptures are addressed to 'the church,' marking the church institute out as higher or *prior in importance* to all other areas of life. But this would be at best a half truth. The Older Testament is not addressed to the church as instituted by the Lord through the disciples, but to all God's people throughout all of history. Moreover, some of it is clearly directed at the unbelieving pagan world, like several of the prophecies of Amos as just one example. The Bible reveals that the Word of God comes to all kinds of men and nations, in all kinds of places, both believers and unbelievers, Jews and Gentiles.

It is true of course that the apostle Paul did not write letters that we know of to Christian schools, political parties or companies (there probably weren't any at the time), but he did address letters to churches (plural). More often, however, his letters are addressed to Christians as saints, that is to believers

(Rom. 1:7; Eph. 1:1; Phil. 1:1; Col. 1:2) and also to individual Christians like Timothy, Titus and Philemon. Only when writing to the Corinthians and Thessalonians are *churches* addressed explicitly. The other letters are addressed simply to Christians, "and as such they are not only church members, but also Christian husbands and wives, Christian parents and children, Christian employers and employees (Eph. 5:22-6:9; Col. 3:18-4:1; 1 Pet. 3:1-7)."[29]

I have taken space to emphasize the importance of distinguishing properly what we mean when speaking about "the church" because if we go astray here, the consequences are far-reaching for cultural and political life. The implication of what I am arguing here is that my local congregation or denomination, if faithful to an orthodox Christian confession, important as it is, is only one small, temporal and visible expression of the universal, transcendent and invisible body over which Christ Himself is absolute head. There can be no question that, as Geerhardus Vos notes, "the kingdom-forces which are at work, the kingdom-life which exists in the invisible sphere, find expression in the kingdom-organism of the visible church."[30] There is mighty kingdom power at work in Christ's instituted church that cannot be ignored, bypassed or minimized in the Christian life. In addition, the authority exercised in faithful churches derives from Christ, not men. However, from this it does not follow, as Vos recognizes, that "the visible church is the only outward expression of the visible kingdom."[31] To borrow a biological metaphor, we can think of the church as *organism* – the universal body of Christ consisting of all believers serving Christ as Lord in *all of life* – and of the locally *instituted* church which includes the specific organization and tasks of church elders, pastors and the various offices as well as the obligations of members of the congregation to each other. This called-out people are then given the task of going out into all the world with both the message and reconciling life of the kingdom of God in the power of the Holy Spirit.

THE CHURCH AND THE KINGDOM

This more precise description of the church highlights both the intimate relation as well as the vital distinction between the church and the kingdom of God. Vos notes that "the conception of the kingdom is common to all periods of our Lord's teaching, that of the church emerges only at two special points of His ministry as recorded in Matthew 16:18 and 18:17."[32] The word for Kingdom in the New Testament is *basileia*. It is the significance and power of this now manifest reality, first organized amongst the disciples by the Lord, that the gospel as a whole has in view. Although occasionally the concepts of the kingdom and the church seem almost parallel (because of their intimate relation), Herman Ridderbos in his classic work *The Coming of the Kingdom* notes:

> [W]e should point out that the concept *basileia* nowhere occurs in the sense of this idea of the *ekklesia*. Nor is it used in the sense that the kingdom of God in its provisional manifestation on earth would be embodied in the form and organization of the church…; by the term kingdom of God

we can denote not only the fulfilling and completing action of God in relation to the entire cosmos, but also various facets of this all-embracing process. Thus, e.g., the territory within which this divine action occurs and in which the blessings of the kingdom are enjoyed is called the *basileia* of God or that of heaven (cf. Matt. 5:20; 11:11; 23:13).[33]

Clearly, the scriptural teaching about *being in* the kingdom of God or *entering* the kingdom of God as a fulfilled reality through Christ is not describing a person's admittance into a temporal, local Christian community. The Bible simply does not use *basileia* in the sense of "church," yet it never minimizes the importance of the church as the new people on mission within the revelation of Christ and His kingdom. The setting aside of empirical Israel as the covenant people and the formation of a new humanity as the seed of Abraham and children of the kingdom is realized in the coming of Christ and is explicitly taught by Him: "Therefore say I unto you, the kingdom of God shall be taken from you, and given to a nation (people) bringing forth the fruits thereof" (Matt. 21:43-46). In short, the salvation of the kingdom is being given to a new people to be gathered in by the messiah. In this context we find both concepts of the kingdom and a new people of God. This called-out people will manifest and bring forth the *fruits of the kingdom*. Church and kingdom therefore are *not* identical. Ridderbos is incisive:

> The *basileia* is the great divine work of salvation in its fulfilment and consummation in Christ; the *ekklesia* is the people elected

and called by God and sharing in the bliss of the *basiliea*. Logically the *basileia* ranks first, and not the *ekklesia*. The former, therefore, has a much more comprehensive content. It represents the all-embracing perspective, it denotes the consummation of all history, brings both grace and judgment, has cosmic dimensions, fills time and eternity. The *ekklesia* in all this is the people who in this great drama have been placed on the side of God in Christ by virtue of the divine election and covenant. They have been given the divine promise, have been brought to manifestation and gathered together by the preaching of the gospel, and will inherit the redemption of the kingdom now and in the great future.[34]

The gathered church remains critical in all of this because "the *ekklesia* is the fruit of the revelation of the *basileia*; and conversely, the *basileia* is inconceivable without the *ekklesia*. The one is inseparable from the other without, however, the one merging into the other."[35] The church then is to be constantly moved, motivated and inspired by the reality that as God's people, the body of Christ, we are chosen instruments of the *basileia* in teaching God's commandments, preaching and applying God's Word to our lives, living out in all its fullness the kingdom charter revealed in Scripture – a charter which demands all things be reconciled to God in Christ (2 Cor. 5:19).

The clear distinction and relation of the church and kingdom of God helps us to recognize several important things. First, it enables us to appreciate and value the important role the church has in its own God-ordained sphere and to be committed to its local visible expression.

Here we worship together, are taught the Word, receive the sacraments, enjoy faithful discipline and care for one another in an accountable community with other believers. Second, it helps us to see that the calling of the Christian believer is much bigger and more comprehensive in scope than participation in the instituted church as a worshipping community. A kingdom vision frees us from misguided ecclesiastical domination and liberates the believer's *entire life in all its aspects,* to be concretely subject to the Lordship of Jesus Christ and His Word – making the totality of the Christian's life in all spheres an instrument of the kingdom of God. As Vos writes:

> [The] kingship of God, as his recognized and applied supremacy, is intended to pervade and control *the whole of human life in all its forms of existence.* This the parable of the leaven plainly teaches. These various forms of human life have each their own sphere in which they work and embody themselves. There is a sphere of science, a sphere of art, a sphere of the family and of the state, a sphere of commerce and industry. Whenever one of these spheres comes under the controlling influence of the principle of the divine supremacy and glory, and this outwardly reveals itself, there we can truly say that the kingdom of God has become manifest.[36]

The detailed application of this is the calling of every believer – that every province of human life and thought be brought under the sway of God's kingdom. Yet critically, as Vos notes, "it was not [Christ's] intention that this result should be reached by making human life in all its spheres subject to the visible church."[37]

THE PROPER RELATION OF CHURCH, STATE, AND SOCIETY

This brings us to our final argument concerning the way in which kingdom life works itself out and the role the church plays in relation to other spheres of life. With the *basileia/ekklesia* distinction in place we can now see more clearly the various errors in regard to the relationship of church and state. I began this chapter by noting a false dilemma that is typically present in modern evangelical thinking regarding Christianity and political life: pursue a return to an ecclesiastical cultural model with a formally or informally established church taking charge in various aspects of cultural and political life, or acknowledge the secular state as the new unifying principle. I have implied that there is in fact a third option implicit in a proper understanding of the nature of the church and the kingdom of God which avoids the false problematics engendering the struggle between these polarizing views.

On this fresh understanding it becomes clear that relating the gospel (*Christianity)* to the various aspects of society does not require relating the *church institute,* its offices and functions, directly or indirectly to everything possible in society – the first position within the false dilemma I have highlighted is thus exposed as in error. The idea that one needs to *churchify* life to express the life of the kingdom of God – the general assumption that Christianizing culture would require churchmen in high political positions, running schools and universities, governing hospitals and charities, and in one way or another inserting the church's offices and functions into as many areas of life as possible is in reality a hangover from the scholastic thought of the medieval era and the ecclesiastical culture of old Christendom.

Historically, as the church's former influence in this regard steadily waned after the Renaissance, more and more spheres of life were being differentiated and appreciated in Western society, like schools and universities, the arts and sciences, clubs and associations etc. The Roman Catholic Church's (scholastic) solution to recognizing these various societal spheres as having a degree of independence, while retaining an ecclesiastical cultural vision, was to posit the principle of *subsidiarity*. Here, a *relative autonomy* is given to various subordinate areas of life while being conceived as parts within the all-encompassing whole of the *state*. However, this natural state is in turn *superseded and shaped* by the church as a *supernatural* institute of grace. The idea was introduced into Catholic social teaching by Bishop Wilhelm Emmanuel von Ketteler of Mainz in the 1850s but was built on an earlier Thomistic understanding of life.[38] Aquinas had viewed the *state* as the all-inclusive total community in the realm of *nature*, embracing all other spheres of societal life in a whole-parts relation. Of course, the state's jurisdiction did not extend to the church as a supernatural domain of grace – the state was only the *portal* to that domain under the church's supervision.

In this model, the family is at the bottom of a hierarchy of communities that culminates in the state, supervised and spiritually overseen by the church. This hierarchical structure is the core principle of *subsidiarity*. This basically pagan view does not recognize or appreciate the *unique character* of the various social spheres of life as ordained by God. There is a vague conception of the 'common good' to be pursued by the state, but no *criterion* for achieving this. Thomism and Romanism certainly do not want to openly embrace state absolutism, but the societal doctrine of subsidiarity provides no theoretical defense against it. As Herman Dooyeweerd explains, the Roman error was locating the necessarily Christian character of a just state in the control of the church institute:

> Its Christian character was not Scripturally sought in the expression of Christ's Kingdom within the inner structure of the state itself, but Roman Catholicism continued to see the inner structure of the state in the old pagan way as the total bond of all natural society, and continued to deduce the principles for political life by 'natural reason' apart from revelation. The state can participate in the realm of grace, not from within but, since it is itself strictly natural, it can do this only by enlisting in the service of the temporal church-institute.[39]

The attempt of the Roman Church to hold together church and state in ecclesiastical union by making the state the all-encompassing *natural* institution, supervised by the church as a *super-natural* one, cannot be justified scripturally and its historic record in providing religious liberty is poor. Yet a version of it has been incorporated into much of modern evangelical thinking. In this evangelical version the state and socio-cultural life are essentially disconnected not only from the church institute, but from God's rule, His Word and His redemptive work altogether, and allowed to go their own way. Ultimately, the principle of subsidiarity is a violation of both a creational and scriptural principal because, "the state does not *grant existence* to any non-state sphere sovereign social entity. It merely has to acknowledge that, on equal footing, there are multiple distinct and sphere sovereign societal entities."[40]

These Romanist and evangelical variations on a theme fail to properly distinguish the church and the kingdom of God, viewing the church as the principal or only agent of that kingdom. However, as we have seen, since the church cannot be conflated with the kingdom of God itself, the instituted historical church (of whichever tradition) does not have the burden of imposing its confession or authority on the state or the rest of society – it does not need to control or ecclesiasticize society by bringing it under its control. The unique spheres of family, state, academy, business etc., are *not* the church, nor are they subordinate *parts* of the church. Critically however, this does *not* mean they are not to be Christian, transformed and shaped by the gospel, the Word of God and Lordship of Christ. It only means they are not required to be under ecclesiastical control. When it comes to political life and society, the church's role is to prophetically propose, not impose its biblical insight for culture.

With regard to the opposite pole in our false dilemma, the tragic knee-jerk reaction of much contemporary evangelicalism to secularization has not been to try and impose its religious confession on political life, but to erroneously assume a need to dissolve any relationship between Christianity, political life and the broader culture. This is done by implicitly or explicitly devaluing creation and culture as a lower or lesser domain of reality and then essentially collapsing the church and the kingdom of God into one another – often identified as a special domain of grace or 'redemptive kingdom.' In rightly recognizing the need to separate church and state in terms of jurisdiction and function, they have effectively separated God, His kingdom and His law-Word from human cultural activity and the exercise of power and authority in the public sphere. Many of the intellectuals sympathetic to this response end up adopting and promoting individualistic and progressive liberal *democracy* as the most suitable political philosophy for preserving freedoms and a minimal right to preach the gospel – a hope collapsing before our eyes in the West. This untenable liberal position tries to hold together two intractably conflicting principles: a radical autonomy of the individual will (the right to sin against God and be a law unto oneself) on the one hand, and the Christian notion of a transcendent moral law and authority on the other. The result has been the flourishing of a naked pagan individualism alongside a sceptical subjectivism. These ideas find institutional expression in a supposedly 'neutral' secular state. Not only is such a state anything but religiously neutral, it gradually undermines all social order and defeats its own purportedly democratic purpose. As K. L. Grasso points out:

> Contemporary liberalism subverts the foundations of democratic government because the thoroughgoing subjectivism towards which liberalism inexorably tends precludes in principle an affirmation of an objective and universally obligatory order of

justice and rights, and the dignity of the human person. The resultant culture of unbridled individualism and subjectivism is scarcely a fertile soil for the cultivation of republican virtues on which democracy depends.[41]

The attempt of so many Christians today to locate in secular liberal democracy a 'Christian' solution to the relationship of faith and culture, Christianity and the state, must be understood in its broader historical context of the false dilemma already highlighted. On the one hand there is fear of a return to the darker days of religious persecution if a distinctly Christian state and political vision is pursued. On the other hand, self-preservation amidst a radical and aggressive re-paganization of culture motivates the desire to adopt a form of public religious and even legal pluralism that would ostensibly allow Christians to 'remain at the table.' In other cases, secular liberal democracy is chosen simply for want of awareness or understanding of a better and authentically scriptural alternative to the unified ecclesiastical culture of former Christendom and the radical cultural and political relativization of the claims of Christ in modern socialistic liberal democracies.

Because in both cases modern Christians mistakenly see the kingdom of God and the church as functionally the same, and because we rightly recognize that not everyone is 'saved' and should not be coerced into being part of the visible church, we have tended to assume that a truly Christian order for political life is rendered inherently impossible unless a given church with its peculiar confession controls and coerces people to think and act 'Christianly.' Since this is obviously unacceptable, the Christianization of culture, including political life, is rejected as unchristian! It is here that we meet the need for a clearly articulated and scripturally grounded Christian political vision that avoids the pitfall of ecclesiastical coercion and domination whilst rejecting the ideological myth of religious neutrality in politics.

Chapter Three:
State Absolutism, Sphere Sovereignty & the Limits of Political Authority

STATE ABSOLUTISM

One of the most remarkable features of the late-modern era has been the strange coalescence of an incessant call for 'total emancipation' from the shackles of alleged oppression with an explicit totalitarian drift in political life. This initially seems contradictory. On one side there is an anarchistic demand for human life and activity, but it is tied to a totalitarian tendency which, in the name of freedom and radical democracy, allows civil government to pursue its task without any *intrinsic limitations*. This perplexing element of life in the West manifests itself in a constant clamouring amongst the people for complete self-determination, equality and self-expression in the name of 'justice,' whilst looking to the state as the appropriate organ to legislate the rights, entitlements and freedoms being demanded into existence.

People increasingly require a total equality, provision, safety and security to be delivered by the state and it is taken practically for granted that the central government must act as the lord and coordinator of all society. The reformed philosopher Jan Dengerink is to the point:

> To [central government] is ascribed a clear supremacy over all other basically non-political groups. In this fashion, we land up squarely, under the banner of absolute freedom and equality, with a typical totalitarian conception of the state. This clearly shows its out-workings in the socio-political activities of various Western democracies, with all of the structural and spiritual leveling that follows from it ... the result is always a heavy-handed bureaucracy, which in practice reduces the individual citizen to a nullity, one in which the technocrats and social planners get the final say ...[42]

This political reality can be identified as a form of liberal democratic socialism and it trends totalitarian: "Abolishing in principle the unique, original responsibility of all kinds of other societal structures, it hands society over to the all-devouring state leviathan."[43] Put differently, the majority of people have become statist in their thinking, implicitly or explicitly. The central meaning of statism is important to note. The presence of an '-ism' should immediately alert the careful thinker to the possibility that there has been an exaggeration of a created and God-ordained structure (in this case the state) into something well beyond its intended function. Fundamentally statism is a political system in which the sphere of civil government exerts substantial, centralized control over much of society, including the economy and various other spheres.

The dominance of statism today means that few people question anymore progressive, redistributive taxation (including inheritance taxes), national minimum wage laws, market interventionism, the suspension of civil liberties by unelected bureaucrats in the name of public health, banking and big corporation bailouts, state control and funding of medicine, education, charity (through various regulations and incentives) and welfare, as well as a large share of the media such as the BBC and CBC. The British National Health Service alone is one of the world's largest employers.[44] The public sector has become so vast that most people have grown accustomed to the state's omnipresence. Britain today is not a country that the famed British Prime Minister Winston Churchill would have imagined emerging from a conflict against state absolutism.

In this brave new world, the church herself is increasingly treated as little more than another social club with no more significance in culture than a cinema or sports team – possibly less. It is easy to forget the fact that there is in our era a regulated state-church in officially communist countries like China, where some of the churches are authorised by the civil government to gather, worship, practice the rites of the church and even preach from (parts of) the Bible. However, the apparent 'liberties' of those state-approved churches are emphatically constrained by government, including subjects they can address from Scripture. They must submit themselves unequivocally to every regulation, recognizing state authority as absolute. It has only been because of faithful pastors and leaders in China standing on the full authority of the Word of God and the sovereignty of Christ the King, that an 'underground' church which refuses to recognize state control over it, has grown. Yet in the West we seem increasingly ready to allow the state to licence, control and regulate the churches, even to the point of locking them down indefinitely and at will if 'public health' functionaries of the state require it, and ceasing pastoral counseling in biblical truth for those struggling with their sexuality.

The explosion of the regulatory state in the last 70 years, and especially over the last 30, reaching into more and more areas of private life and civil society, is rooted in the idea of the omni-competence of the state and its bureaucracy. Neither Scripture nor Christian historical thought well into the early twentieth century ever envisions such a freedom-sapping behemoth overtaking life. Today, there is no end to the tens of thousands of state regulations to be obeyed in the anglosphere in numerous departments of life. As I found out after a recent move, there are permits required for almost every kind of renovation activity on private property (including the size and colour of garden sheds or moving a bathroom sink) as well as detailed regulations covering the uses of one's property. There are permits and regulations for working from a home office, as well as onerous worksite and office regulations. In fact, the regulations in Western nations are so diverse they cover everything from the size and shape of bananas, the length of nails required in drywall and who is allowed to feed pigs. More regulations require permits for collecting rags and metal and others control games on private premises. Various bylaws mandate the number of parking spaces required per seat in church sanctuaries (Toronto) and liquor stores are barred from selling refrigerated water or soda (Indiana). The list is literally endless and frequently absurd.

This 'omni-competent' vision of the state has become so ubiquitous that many evangelical Christians have lost their cultural memory of God-given, pre-political institutions, rights and responsibilities that are to be protected but are not created, controlled or governed by the state. As a consequence, believers have floundered in their response to unprecedented and illegal lockdowns of the church, the growing collapse of civil liberties, the total control of education, expanded abortion, euthanasia, no-fault divorce law, the redefinition of marriage and family, homosexuality and transgender issues, largely because a scriptural world and life view norming our understanding of these questions and the role of the state with respect to them has collapsed. Instead, we have a liberal democratic and statist worldview drilled into us by the various organs of cultural life, where Jesus and a hope of heaven is spread on top as a sort of spiritual condiment giving religious flavor to secularism via the ministry of the churches.

What has become increasingly clear in recent decades is that we are entering an era (likely protracted) of struggle for the freedom of the church in the West, not just with the state and its bureaucracy, but with various church movements themselves, some of whose leaders are emerging as committed apologists for statism. There has never been a shortage of cultural leaders ready to support and advise falling down before the image of the absolutist state when the music plays – to obey the state elites without question – it is always the Daniels and his three friends ready to pray despite the king's edict, or refusing to bow down to overreaching political power, who are in short supply. As a result, when it comes to analysing threats to freedom from their own civil government, courts and bureaucracy, Christians are generally poorly equipped. Like the proverbial frog slowly boiled to death for failing to detect the rising temperature of the water, we are sleepwalking toward tyranny.

THE SOVEREIGNTY OF GOD

This state of affairs is not just a problem; it is a tragedy, because it is the abandonment of the *legacy of the reformation* which gradually gave us both the free English national church and eventually liberty for non-conformity (Toleration Act, 1689), giving shape to the political life of the entire anglosphere. Abraham Kuyper, an heir of the same reformed tradition on the continent of Europe and who for a time served as Prime Minister of the Netherlands – a country with one of the richest legacies of Christian freedom from the time of William of Orange[45] – has pointed out that:

> The dominating principle [of the Calvinistic side of the reformation] was not, soteriologically, justification by faith, but in the widest sense cosmologically, the *Sovereignty of the Triune God over the whole Cosmos, in all its spheres and kingdoms*, visible and invisible.[46]

This meant emphatically that the state, as well as the church, is ordained of God and under His authority as His servant (Prov. 8:15-16; Rom. 13:1ff). In Romans 13, Paul specifically and explicitly places all authority under God – including civil government – as a sphere of power and authority instituted by Him alone. The apostle's prescription concerning the state's task as well as his exhortation against resisting God's order in temporal authority, assumes that to do so resists God's command and so he presupposes the absolute sovereignty of God.

What is clearly at issue for Paul in Romans 13 is man's propensity to resist God's ordinances and commands. Clearly, we cannot selectively obey God's commands at our convenience – including recognizing the legitimacy of temporal authority. All God's commands and ordinances need to be considered and obeyed. This being the case, if the state presumes to forbid what God commands, or commands what God forbids, the state has moved beyond its delimited authority and those who obey God must at that point resist such arrogant presumption. This is clear in the chapter as Paul goes on to teach that the civil authority is God's servant – which literally means God's deacon. The apostle explains that this entails being a terror to bad conduct and approving of good conduct, bearing the sword to avenge those that do wrong. But if the state becomes a terror to those who do good and rewards those who do evil, it is again in flagrant violation of God's command and ordinance, and Christians have at that point a duty to resist an authority that has ceased to be God's deacon. This explains why Paul spent so much time in prison and in the courts himself because he was deemed to be resisting authority. Were this not the case, we would be bound to state absolutism with no basis for resistance to tyranny of any and every kind. So, we are to obey God's ordinance to submit to civil authorities and fulfil our obligations until the state moves against God's norms and ordinances. In all other cases we obey for the sake of our conscience and to avoid unnecessary punishment.

For centuries this had been the dominant Christian view. As James Willson wrote in his outstanding commentary on Romans 13 in 1853, nothing can nullify the law of God: "To the best government, obedience can be yielded only in things lawful; for there is a "higher law" to which rulers and subjects are alike amenable. "The heavens do rule." There is a God above us, and "to Him every knee shall bow, and every tongue shall confess that Jesus Christ is Lord, to the glory of God the Father."[47] Willson shows in great detail how Paul demonstrates that "God alone is the source of legitimate authority. He is sovereign. Man is His. Power, not derived from God is ever illegitimate. It is mere usurpation."[48] In particular, Willson is diligent to expose the misuse of Romans 13 as a text promoting passive obedience and non-resistance in the face of evil and rebellion against God:

> Paul did not intend by the language before us, to forbid even the forcible resistance of unjust and tyrannical civil magistrates, not even when that resistance is made with the avowed design of displacing offending rulers, or, it may be, the change of the very form of government itself...That question was settled in England by the revolution of 1688, when the nation, rising in

its might, expelled James II as an enemy to the constitutional rights and liberties of the people. The separate national and independent existence of these United States is the fruit of successful revolution.[49]

In 1 Timothy 2:1-2, Christians are also urged by the apostle Paul to pray and intercede for kings and those in authority. Contrary to implying some sort of unquestioning subservience, this command reveals the *high mediatorial position* of the believer and Christ's instituted church. The believer is required to go to the sovereign ruler of the kings of the earth (Rev. 1:5), because of our status as a royal priesthood and holy nation before God (1 Pt. 2:9) and intercede for mercy and wisdom (or indeed judgment) to be upon earthly rulers, in order that God's people be left in peace and freedom to live godly lives. In short, believers are to use their high position before the Lord so that they can be *left alone by civil authorities*, to serve the kingdom of God.

This perspective on God's sovereignty constitutes the root of religious liberty, freedom of conscience and indeed true *political liberty* in the West. From the Christian standpoint, there is no absolute power or authority for Parliament, civil governments or monarchs. All authority is delegated, limited and under God in the various God-ordained spheres of life. In light of this, and because of the legitimate sword power given to the state, Kuyper rightly warns, "*we must ever watch against the danger which lurks, for our personal liberty, in the power of the state.*"[50] And he keeps the state in check by likewise asserting the absolute authority of God alone:

From the ends of the earth God cites all nations and peoples before His high judgment seat. For God created the nations. They exist for Him. They are His own. And therefore, all these nations, and in them humanity, must exist for His glory and consequently after His ordinances, in order that in their well-being, when they walk after His ordinances, His divine wisdom may shine forth ... this right is possessed by God, and by Him alone. No man has the right to rule over another man, otherwise such a right necessarily and immediately becomes the right of the strongest ... nor can a group of men, by contract, from their own right, compel you to obey a fellow man ... authority over men cannot arise from men. Just as little from a majority over against a minority.[51]

To say the least, this is not the prevailing view among professing Christians today. The spirit of the French Revolution and German philosophical pantheism permeating the West's social democracies opposes God and recognizes no ground for a just state or political authority in anything other than man himself. *"No God, no master"* was a matter of confession for the French revolutionaries. On this view, all power and authority proceeds from man alone. Thus, the *absolute* sovereignty of the people or the state is confessional and practical atheism. This is not what the English constitutional arrangements had in mind with the idea of the sovereignty of Parliament, since it is the monarch's Parliament, and elected leaders are *invited* by the monarch to form a government. The Head of State of the United Kingdom and Canada swears an oath, under the absolute sovereignty of Christ the King, to uphold the law and gospel of Christ and to defend that faith once for all delivered to the saints. State omnipotence then, is the opposite of biblical teaching (Dan. 2:21-24; Acts 17:7) and runs contrary to the history of the English Revolution and the legacy of the mother of all parliaments. On Oliver Cromwell's tomb at Westminster Abbey, we read the epitaph (the battle cry of the Puritans), *"Christ not man is King."*

SPHERE SOVEREIGNTY

It is evident then that a scripturally rooted solution is required that addresses head-on the present crisis of social order and the relationship of Christianity to political and cultural life that doesn't fall into the false dilemma dealt with in the previous chapter – a choice between a unified ecclesiastical culture or a totally relativized place for the claims of Christ and His church in a secularized order. Any solution will be inadequate if it merely *appreciates* and respects the historic separation of the jurisdictions of church and state. It must realize that *all spheres of life* – family, church, state, academy, professional associations and bodies, economic life and business, art, science, and all else besides – are themselves, in their own spheres, to be made subject to the Lordship of Christ and the Word of God, as equally important aspects of the *kingdom of God.* This creational and kingdom principle (Gen 1:28-31; 1 Cor 10:26, 31; Col 3:17) is the polar opposite of the pagan notion of the *total state* and the syncretistic idea of *subsidiarity* which seeks to Christianize the pagan ideal. As Dooyeweerd has explained:

Neither marriage, nor family, nor blood-relation, nor the free types of social existence, whether they are organized or not, can be considered as *part* of an all-embracing state. Every societal relationship has received from God its own structure and law of life, sovereign in its own sphere. The Christian world and life view, illumined by the revealed Word of God, posits sphere sovereignty of the temporal life spheres over against the pagan totality idea.[52]

The basic creational principle at work here (Col. 1:15-20; Rev. 1:5) was first called *sphere sovereignty* by Abraham Kuyper. The fundamental teaching of sphere sovereignty rests on four essential biblical principles. The first, as already discussed, is the total sovereignty of God over all of creation which He called into existence (Ps. 103:19; Prov. 16:4). Because of the providence of God active at every moment, He also guides the development or becoming of His creation in the unfolding of its potentiality. As such, His sovereign providence is a constant and absolute (Job 1:21; Ps. 75:6-7; Prov. 3:6; Dan 4:35; Matt. 10:29; Acts 17:26; Rom. 11:36). No area of life is exempt from the authority of the creator and redeemer (1 Chron. 29:11).

Secondly, all social institutions in their historical disclosure, despite the distortions and disturbance present due to the fall into sin, find their ultimate origin in creation since everything was separated and distinguished 'after its kind' in creation, having the right to exist and develop (Gen. 1; 1 Cor. 15:38-41; Eph. 3:14-15). Thirdly, God's authority is a lawful authority. Though He is above law and not bound by it, as the author of all creation He governs His creatures by law and promises His covenant faithfulness to that law-word. God's law-Word is refracted within creation into a vast plurality of forms – i.e., for the inorganic and organic world, as well as the total life of man in all his functions and institutions. These laws, norms and ordinances of creation can be studied and understood, and they express the will of God for creation, providing order and constancy and obligating creatures in all their life activities (1 Kings 4:29-34; Ps. 119; Eccl. 1:4-10; Is. 28:23-29). Fourthly and finally, because of God's laws for creation, each person and social institution has the right to exist alongside others with a duty to function in terms of God's Word in creation and Scripture, being obligated to fulfil a specific task and calling in history in terms of God's kingdom (Gen. 1:28; 22:18; Ps. 1; Eccl. 12:13; Matt: 7:26; John 14:21; Rom. 2:6-11):[53]

> The laws of creation, therefore, make possible a plurality of social institutions or spheres, each with a measure of autonomy or sovereignty vis-à-vis all others. The sovereignty of any social sphere, however, is always limited by the sovereignty of co-existing spheres and limited to the task or function to which it is called. Moreover, this earthly sovereignty is subservient to the absolute sovereignty of God. It is delegated by God and remains ever dependent upon Him.[54]

On this view, by virtue of God's creation ordinances and laws for cultural development there are varied differentiated spheres of life within human society including the family, church, state, business, educational institutions, the arts and so forth, which do not *owe their existence* to the state, nor do they *derive their internal sphere of law* from the state. These spheres of life must obey the authority of God and His Word over them. They are not subservient to the state, nor do they relate to the state in *parts-to-whole fashion* as though they were lesser 'parts' of the state. As such the state has no right to overreach and intrude into them. The parts of the state proper are provinces and municipalities, unified under one public legal order within a given territory. Families, churches, schools, businesses etc., may reside and function in that territory, but that does make those entities *parts* of the state.

On this model each sphere is prevented from dominating, controlling and absorbing each other. Instead, each area of life (including the family, church and state) enjoys an internal sovereignty. God has established these various spheres of life to be governed in terms of their own structural principles, ruled by His Word and subject ultimately to Christ as Lord and king. The state does not *grant existence* to the family or the church as though they were lesser parts of itself. Instead, the state must recognize their uniqueness, acknowledge the legitimacy of their relative independence and respect the boundaries of their God-given freedom and authority. This important principle cuts both ways. The church institute does not *grant authority* to the state by directly appointing or anointing it. As Kuyper explains:

> When the state and government are bound to God by a bond *of their own*, even before the church of Christ was there and also without her involvement, then the result is the natural,

simplest, and, in comparison with other systems, the most desirable relation of church and state. It is not the church that hands the sceptre to the government…; in the days when Christ was on earth, before his apostles established his churches, Christ himself testified to Pontius Pilate that the power wielded by the Roman emperor and his governor was power given to them by God.[55]

Importantly, this direct accountability of the state to God does not set aside the obligation of churches to preach righteousness in the public space and to prophetically speak truth to power. Nor does it diminish the responsibility of *all Christians* in *every area of life* and culture to diligently apply their faith and the fulness of the Word of God – whether they are lawyers, politicians, judges, teachers, artists or mechanics. As Kuyper put it, "If one at this point asks whether the Christian religion should not also influence public life, the answer is: without a doubt…; but that influence must come to expression along the constitutional route."[56]

Our secular culture, in the hope of doing away with laws and norms for creation, has invariably tried to reduce human social organization and relationships to bare 'natural facts' with merely biological, psychological and economic causal explanations for their existence. But human social relations are not discerned in the same way that we can observe the causal relations in the behavior of a flock of geese – that is, they are not given to us as empirical natural facts. The various typical structures that allow us to distinguish different forms of human social relationship (e.g., family, church and state) are intangible and so the natural sciences cannot discover them. Attempts to 'explain' social structures without creational norms end up explaining nothing. As Dooyeweerd makes clear:

> The state, church, family, marriage, and commercial enterprise, as well as social classes, ranks, and others are not entities that one can weigh and measure. They are not objectively presented to one's sensory perception. One cannot discern or understand them without the application of norms or criteria of propriety. For the very existence of these social relations depends upon these norms, even though in their actual functioning these relations may conflict with such norms. Even the actual activity of a gang of thieves cannot be recognized as such without the application of the norms of an ordered society ... we can never discuss factual social relations in human society without discussing real social norms, even when these relations violate the norms. This also implies it is impossible for sociologists to give a causal explanation without reference to social norms ... if we try to make a consistent attempt to eliminate normative criteria, we shall discover that we end up with no real *human* social facts.[57]

Although the de-Christianizing cultures of the West have sought to shake free from God's revelation in creation and Scripture which delimit the life and institutions of people in terms of normative laws – like logical norms for thought, laws and norms for language, social order, economics, moral and legal life etc., – we find that they are inescapable and cannot be set aside without chaos ensuing. The attempt to be lawless, normless, is entirely self-defeating. The idea of a feeling for justice or a sense of injustice, for example immediately presupposes normativity. To be human is to be a creature aware of laws and norms that govern our lives in every sphere.

That is obviously not to say that throughout history human beings have positivized (applied and made concrete) God's laws and norms faithfully. Because of sin and rebellion against God, cultural development is shaped by a constant and continual conflict between normative (faithful) and anti-normative (unfaithful) religious motives pulling culture, social structures and relationships in different directions. Just consider today the denial of creational normativity for human identity and sexuality and the consequent efforts to redefine the social and legal structures of marriage and family. In addition, the progress of redemption and historical revelation has opened human eyes in new ways to God's will and purpose so that our understanding is deepened regarding God's law-order. As such, human understanding of the normative role and function of human government has varied and been subject to historical disclosure. Powerful forces driven by deep religious convictions have frequently pushed human society in a totalitarian direction:

> As a religious-political community, the Greek polis [city-state] was totalitarian in nature. It knew nothing of either the modern concept of freedom of certain spheres of life – which as a matter of principle are withdrawn from the state's control – or of the distinction between state and society. Thus, both Plato and Aristotle treated all sociological questions with the framework of the *politica*, the theory of the polis.[58]

Although a synthesis between the pagan view of the Greco-Roman world and Christianity was attempted in the Holy Roman Empire in the ninth century, biblical faith, especially through the reformation, provided an alternative view for understanding human society:

> It is the theme of creation, fall into sin, and redemption by Christ Jesus in the communion of the Holy Spirit. It reveals that the religious community of the human race is rooted in creation, in the solidarity of the fall into sin, and in the spiritual kingdom of God through Christ Jesus (the Corpus Christi). In this belief Christianity destroys in principle any claim made by a temporal community to encompass all of human life in a totalitarian sense. It demands internal independence for the church in its relation to the state and sharpens our view of the proper nature of the spheres of life.[59]

The principle of sphere sovereignty thus enables us to distinguish a *just state* from an absolutist *power state*, because a just state will recognize, in terms of the Christian principle, a variety of *spheres of law* within society including *public law, civil private law and non-civil private law*. Public or constitutional law concerns the constitution, penal law and laws of criminal procedure as well as administrative law – these are meant to guarantee our political freedoms. Common law, or civil private law, exists to guarantee our freedom of thought and expression, association and so forth, making sure that as individuals and social entities we are on an equal footing with others. Critically, non-civil private law concerns the existence and freedom of non-political spheres of law, like the church. Prior to the historical-cultural differentiation of the different spheres of law beginning in the West with the life of the church institute as independent of the state, undifferentiated societies did not know an independent church, school, or state. Undeveloped societal forms of the extended family, clan, sib and tribe sought to fulfill in an undifferentiated way the tasks and functions of the distinct societal forms we know today. The recognition of distinct spheres of law in Western society is the result of a drawn-out historical process and requires the existence of a genuine state (*res publica*) with an independent and impartial judiciary where decisions are executed by officers of the state.

Public law or constitutional law is communal law with its own distinct character:

> It comprehends the legal organisation and arrangement of relationships of authority and compliance between government and subjects. This organisation is founded on the sword power of the government and is intended to bring to expression the public legal idea of the common good.[60]

This public or constitutional law is distinct from the domain of *civil private law* which involves the regulation of private relationships that do not involve authority and subordination. Here the significance and worth of image-bearers as *individuals* is given legal expression regardless of ethnicity, sex, or personal beliefs – it is the asylum of the individual person. Dooyeweerd explains the existence of civil private law:

It presupposes a high degree of differentiation and integration of legal life and is geared to one structure in human society only, namely that of coordinational civil relationships that fall outside the internal communal and collective spheres of marriage, family, the business firm, organisations, and so on, thus to relationships in which individuals do not exercise any authority over one another … it presupposes the development of individualized private societal relationships where people participate in coordinated interaction as individual legal subjects with juridical equality. Distinct from the specific private communal law obtaining within particular societal collectivities such as the family, church, school, business, social club, etc., the sole purpose of civil law is to apply the demands of social justice in the reciprocal private interactions between individuals.[61]

Clearly, none of the jural spheres of human society can exist in isolation. The civil law-sphere is obviously intertwined with the state, but it is *not* communal public law. Neither should it be equated with non-civil private law (or private communal law) manifest in the distinct structures of marriage and family, the extended family, the private school, voluntary associations and organizations and the business corporation. Law falling outside of the domain of public law is not all private *civil* law, because private law includes various spheres of law which do not have a civil-legal character. Civil private law thus needs to be balanced by the non-civil private law of private communities which should defend their own sphere sovereignty against encroachment by the state:

What falls outside the domain of civil law is all the specific law of private communities and collectivities which serve their inner structure, guided by a destination lying outside the jural domain. This is the case in internal marriage and family law, internal business law, internal associational law, internal church law, and so on.[62]

This means, for example, that the civil magistrate cannot command or interpret the proper nature of church discipline, doctrine or worship, because this is the domain of non-civil private law and lies outside of the state's competency. It also means that, where civil private law or public law does 'touch' on these non-civil private spheres of authority – say, in the marriage relationship – it does so only with respect to its *external* private civil or public side i.e., the marriage contract/ licence and divorce law, or criminal matters in cases of violence or abuse. And the same is true in regard to the church if clergy were assaulting or abusing members. This limitation on the state is necessary because marriage, as an intimate societal form, functions in numerous *internal* relationships like husband and wife, parent and child etc.

Abraham Kuyper explores the institution of the family as a crucial example of a private law-sphere which by virtue of its very existence and ordination of God limits the state:

> The sphere of the family opens itself, with its right of marriage, domestic peace, education and possession; and in this sphere also the natural head is conscious of exercising an inherent

authority – *not because the government allows it,* but because God has imposed it. Paternal authority roots itself in the very life-blood and is proclaimed in the fifth commandment ... Calvinism protests against state-omnipresence; against the horrible conception that no right exists above and beyond existing laws; and against the pride of absolutism...[63]

This delimiting principle is absolutely vital because most people tend to think of all law as *state law* and all government as *state government.* Yet in terms of the scriptural idea of sphere sovereignty (that is, spheres of law), the state (that is, civil government) is only one form of human government and no state has a legitimate right or authority to invade other law-spheres and redefine pre-political societal structures like the family and marriage (let alone biological and creational realities like human sexuality), or to dictate to the church institute how she will worship and govern her members. The same applies to the question of how and what private schools and home schools should teach their children, how a person should decide and conduct their business investments and transactions, or what the artist should paint, or the musician compose and perform. The state only has a valid interest in these matters if and when crimes are being committed or infractions of civil private law come into view. In other words, "Dominion is exercised everywhere," as Kuyper argued, "but it is a dominion which works organically, not by virtue of a state investiture, but from life's sovereignty itself."[64] Thus, the church does not exist by the permission of civil government any more than the family is created by the state. The church is governed and ruled by Jesus Christ under His Word. The state cannot command the church not to preach Christ, baptise or administer the sacraments and exercise church discipline, because Christ Himself and His inspired apostles gave these commands (Matt. 28:16-20; 1 Cor. 11:23-32).

Danie Strauss has pointed out the implications of all this for a Christian view of political life – a just state *must account* for political, communal and personal freedoms. He writes:

> These forms of freedom are correlated with three irreducible jural spheres, namely the sphere of public law, civil private law and non-civil private law. If they are threatened or abolished, we meet a totalitarian and absolutistic state (a power state which is the opposite of a just state), with no guarantees for any form of religious freedom … the Kingdom message of the New Testament, opens up a dynamic cultural-historical process of differentiation and disclosure in which the state emerges as guided by its sphere-sovereign juridical qualification, alongside a multiplicity of non-political societal entities with their own intrinsic competence to form (non-state) law. When Christians assume responsibility for the unfolding of human societal relationships, the public legal order of the state will not threaten, but protect religious freedom…[65]

It is clear to even the casual observer that Western states today are steadily seeking to abolish the irreducibility of these spheres of law by overreaching into the life of the family, the church institute, the school and business, medicine, private charities and more. This is done primarily by seeking to bring each area of society directly or indirectly under the total control of the state, making them parts or sub-domains of the sphere of public law. Life, sexuality, marriage and historic freedoms are being redefined by unelected judiciaries in the name of Charters and Constitutions (public law), while concurrently, laws are gradually introduced into public criminal or civil codes by an ignorant (and at times malevolent) legislature that undermine personal freedoms historically protected by private civil law, which then also results in the rapid disappearance of the freedoms of the family, church, school and business. In short, the sphere of public law is incrementally eating up the private spheres of law altogether. Increasingly, the citizen stands denuded before the total state, stripped of the protection of mediating non-civil private institutions and even of the inherited liberties of private civil law.

This foreboding totalitarian drift exposes the re-paganization of the Western view of the state – a logical consequence of the dechristianization of culture. The biblical perspective stands in radical contrast: government expressed in the state is not to be "ruling over the nation for its own profit, but as a God-ordained power to guard the interests of the nation and to honor God in the nation."[66] This implies that each God-ordained sphere of life, created by His Word, is obligated to submit itself to Christ by honoring and respecting each law-sphere and keeping within the limits established by God. None of this is to say that the state does not have an important and legitimate role under the sovereignty of God and His Word. But the church, the family, the school and other spheres have their own king, and it isn't the state. As Kuyper puts it in regard to the church institute, "Her position in the state is not assigned her by the permission of the Government, but *Jure divino.* She has her own organisation. She possesses her own office-bearers ... the sovereignty of the State and the sovereignty of the Church exist side by side, and they mutually limit each other."[67]

ECCLESIOCRACY OR THEOCRACY?

The political implication of sphere sovereignty is thus unequivocally theocratic in the sense that there is no part of the cosmos, no law-sphere, no aspect of society or culture that is not being made subject to the Lord Jesus Christ and His Word. The family, the church, the school, the courts, parliament or congress are all called to be expressions, however fallibly, of the *basileia* of God. It is this view of politics alone that protects us from absolutizing and thereby deifying some form of political life. Willem Ouweneel is incisive:

> In socialism, the state is deified; in libertarianism, the individual; in communism the party; and in national socialism, the nation is deified. Only in a truly biblical situation, the state as well as the individual, the party as well as the nation, are directed toward God. We do not serve the state, but the state and we are to serve God ... therefore, every nation state that in principle and in practice, functions out of the acknowledgment of Christ's kingship, also within political life, is a manifestation, no matter how weak, of the kingdom of God.[68]

It is sometimes objected that this kingdom vision of sphere sovereignty under the supreme potentate, Jesus Christ, would *require* some form of establishment – that one church denomination or another must necessarily have its particular confession established and *imposed* if the state is to be genuinely Christian. It is then concluded that to avoid this injustice and potential for persecution of dissenters, we are better off with a secular 'neutral' state pursuing a vague notion of the 'common good' rather than seeking a Christian state that listens to the Word of God.

The neutral state ideal among Christians is influenced by the modernism of both Karl Barth and Emil Brunner. Barth saw the state as a neutral instrument where religious tolerance is the ultimate wisdom[69] and Brunner rejected both abiding creational norms and Holy Scripture as the direct Word of God binding men and nations – the influence of Gnosticism on Brunner in particular is clear.[70] Yet the notion that a Christian state must involve the establishment of a particular church institution is evidently fallacious thinking for several reasons. First of all, as we have already seen, it fails to recognize the true nature of the church in Scripture in its relationship to the *kingdom of God* and continues to think in scholastic terms inherited from pagan Greek thought:

> Paganism, unable to transcend time, seeks a last and highest temporal bond of which all other societal relationships can be no more than dependent parts. *Christianity does not place a temporal church institute above the state as an ultimate bond,* but in Christ it looks beyond time toward the total theocracy,

the invisible church of Christ. Here, all temporal societal relationships are rooted and grounded, and each of these, after its own divine structure and God-given law, must be an expression, be it an imperfect one, of that invisible kingdom of God. This basic Christian idea of the kingdom of God is the only possible ground for the Christian idea of the state.[71]

Second, it is inescapable that the state as a societal institution, like all other areas of life, functions in the faith aspect of human experience, making neutrality not just an undesirable but impossible ideal. A democratic state which installs its government through a voting process is run by an elected differentiated public who all bring their *beliefs, convictions and moral commitments* to their work and service. The notion of the 'common good' to be pursued by the state is not self-explanatory and cannot be left as a contentless abstraction, for the question immediately arises, what is the 'good' and how is that to be determined? The reality is that the dominant faith and worldview underlying a culture is a spiritual motive force giving shape to the public life of the state. The naïve idea of a neutral state pursuing a harmony of legal interest in the public square whilst not endorsing both explicitly and implicitly some conception of what is true and good within its laws, constitutional liberties, conception of rights and promotion of justice and fairness, is a mirage. As such, when faithful Christians bring biblical faith to bear in public office, the activity of the state in their orbit would necessarily reflect the impact of Christian principles. When committed secularists and pagans do the same, the state's activity will reflect their principles.

Thirdly, in order for the very concept of Christianity to exist (and therefore the idea of a Christian state), a *mere Christianity* must be definable. There is no reason whatsoever to require that one tradition or sectarian confession be imposed by the state to the exclusion of all the others. All genuinely Christian denominations in the West have for centuries shared in common the ecumenical creeds (Apostles' and Nicene) as a fundamental point of agreement. They have also all regarded (until the invasion of liberalism in the late nineteenth century) the Bible as the Word of God. It is on this ecumenical basis that one could speak of a Christian state led by genuinely Christian faith.

In this regard, it is important to note the difference between *ecclesiastical* confession of faith and *political* confession of faith. The state does not need to 'take a position' on internal ecclesiastical matters such as forms of church government, modes of baptism, confessional tradition, or charismatic gifts. Those are theological developments within various church traditions that are outside of the competency of the state (as a public *legal* order) to address. The church institute is qualified and led by the *faith* aspect (law-sphere) of our experience and is concerned with its confession of faith and rites as a believing community. The state is qualified *juridically* and is concerned with the legal order. The Christian state can recognize and affirm in its public communal manifestations (i.e., in its prayers, anthems and constitution) the Lordship of Christ, the foundational creeds of the historic church and the authority of God's law-Word, without being Baptist, Presbyterian, Roman, or any other denomination. And the legislature can listen (as a legislative body, not as a church body) to the Word of God and the prophetic witness of God's people in faithfully positivizing law in light of Scripture – as the Western tradition has done from the time of King Alfred the Great. In this fashion the state can perform a Christian political integrating function in the faith-life of the nation in cultures where the people are marked by a broadly Christian commitment.[72]

Fourth, professing Christian nation states have existed and continue to exist which, however attenuated, have not imposed any particular church's confession. Both Canada and the United States are good examples of historically Christian nations with no federally established church. Even in England where there is now a 'soft establishment,' there has been toleration of all Christian denominations for centuries. Though secularism, humanism and paganism have grown rapidly in North America in the last sixty years and in general the number of committed church-going Christians is in decline, Canada was established as a Christian dominion with a national motto drawn from Psalm 72:8. Even its modern Charter of Rights and Freedoms from 1982 began with a preamble recognizing the supremacy of God. The United States of America, which formally separates church and state (at the Federal level), is possibly the most Christian nation the world has ever known – one nation, under God, as originally conceived. The President still takes his oath of office on the Bible – it used to be taken on a Bible opened to Deuteronomy 27-28 which invokes God's blessing and cursing on a nation for obedience and disobedience. It is therefore demonstrably false to equate the idea of a Christian state or nation with establishment, persecution or the necessity of imposing one church's unique confession on a nation. It was for these reasons, and especially in view of the principle of sphere sovereignty, that Kuyper, over a century ago, lauded the situation in the United States:

> Not a single country can be found in Europe where the relation of state and church is more blessed than in the United States. The national government honors God, does not meddle in ecclesiastical disputes, and is free to set its own course. Conversely, the church of Christ, far from being an obstacle, instead satisfies life's needs with the richest variety, has a place of honor throughout the entire land, is financially independent, and influences public opinion (and through it the president and Congress); it does so to such a degree that no European national church can even begin to be compared with the powerful influence of America's churches on the life of the nation. The churches do not hinder the state in any way, and the state does not place any obstacle in the way of the church's life. Both have complete autonomy and independence.[73]

Naturally, as the United States has seen progressive decline in those confessing the Christian faith, corresponding de-Christianization in culture and growing threats to the freedom of the church politically have developed. The American system was designed for a Christian people, so if the nation continues to wander from the faith, their system of government will continue to steadily come apart.

Nonetheless, Kuyper was right in noting the immeasurable benefits of a free church, in a free nation, that recognizes and honors God. In such a situation no sole church confession is imposed, and godly laws and liberty are among the many fruits of life lived in light of the Word of God. Historically, both Canada and the United States have much to be thankful for in this regard, and much now hangs in the balance. Where a Christian confession among the people is lost, the freedom of the church institute and God's people in every cultural arena will inevitably decline with it. Our era is therefore one of great danger and also of great opportunity. Which one it becomes for the generations that follow very much depends on our level of commitment to the Lordship of Christ today.

THE COERCIVE CHARACTER OF THE STATE

Throughout this short book I have argued that the principle of *sphere sovereignty*, which is rooted in the Lordship of Christ and authority of His Word, provides the template for organizing a biblical political philosophy, a principle of *resistance* to absolutism, totalitarianism and tyranny. The present cultural situation in the West clearly manifests the urgent need for the recovery of a *distinctly Christian* view of the state in which believers are ready and willing to reckon with the state's inescapably religious character.

The thought of an openly religious state, and the idea of principled resistance to unjust civil authority, will be jarring to the sensibilities of many modern evangelicals. However, I believe this is the clear biblical position. Furthermore, it will not do to say that the perspective I have delineated is just one among many possible and legitimate views of the state available to Christians – allowing us to complacently fall back on the secular liberal status quo and baptise its pagan conceptions as Christian. The principles I have outlined should not be regarded as simply an eccentric or parochial view emerging from Calvinists in the Netherlands and English puritans that we can take or leave depending on our cultural taste and heritage. As Dooyeweerd observed:

> We must protest when other views, which reject this sphere sovereignty because they have compromised with pagan philosophy, are considered as at least comparable Christian views. There is only one Christian view concerning human relationships which indeed takes seriously, without compromise, the scriptural principle of the kingdom of God.[74]

This point becomes very evident when we notice the consequences of setting the scriptural principle of the kingdom of God aside. If we violate sphere sovereignty and, in secular liberal fashion, bring the properly coercive sword-power of the state into all the organs and institutions of societal life, the character of human society radically changes because the various structures that make up its great diversity are hindered or completely prevented from serving the kingdom of God within their own law-sphere. In such a case, the lordship of Christ over them is explicitly or implicitly denied. This problem is magnified tenfold when the state itself loses its moorings in the Christian tradition and instead of maintaining only an *external* and *extensive* relationship to the other spheres of life (touching only their public legal relations and preventing violations of sphere sovereignty), seeks to become *internal* and *intensive* in relation to all the structures of society, reforming them as lesser parts of the state itself.

For example, if a secular liberal civil government runs and funds the sphere of *education* today you get radical secularization and the imposition of LGBTQ curriculum and neo-Marxist socio-political indoctrination in schools – like it or not. If you bring state power into the pre-political sphere of *family*, you get the redefinition of marriage, bans on discipline and the sexualization and seizure of our children as the state assumes the role of parent – and in some nations like Canada will remove children if state 'therapies' enforcing queer theory are not implemented with confused minors. If you bring government into the sphere of *welfare provision and charity*, you cultivate a radical dependency on an ever-expanding welfare state, undermine the family, promote entitlement and sponsor statist redistribution of wealth in the form of socialism along with the steady collapse of real charity. If you bring the state into the heart of the *church Institute*, you get a politicized and regulated church that is unwilling or unable to speak the truth of the gospel and Christ's lordship to political authorities, and frequently, religious persecution. If you bring the state into the heart of the economic sphere with interventionism in free markets, heavy regulation and a burgeoning state bureaucracy employing vast numbers of people, you get socialist collectivism with a 'planned' economy – including minimum wage laws, price fixing and fiat currency with quantitative easing – powerful unions and the steady demise of the free market. If you bring the state into the heart of *medicine* you get medicalized technocratic social planning, coercive state-funded abortion, coercive state-funded euthanasia, state-funded sex-change surgery, the denial of the conscience rights of doctors and the indefinite suspension of civil liberties with the mass lockdown of society in the name of *public health* and saving the institutions of socialized medicine (like Britain's National Health Service and Canada's Ontario Health Insurance Plan). If you bring the civil government into the heart of *media* through state-funded broadcasting and state control you get government media, manipulation of the public narrative, an attack on the free press, various hate speech codes and the attempt to control the dissemination of approved information. All of this control and coercion is inevitable when the state moves beyond its sphere of competency and authority into other sovereign spheres because the state, by its very God-ordained nature, is a *coercive* institution. This is why the state must be delimited by the creational principle of sphere sovereignty. Without this limitation, the state inevitably trends totalitarian, bringing its sword power wherever it goes, in terms of its ideological agenda.

The quasi-religious character of the 'statism' prevalent in the modern West should thus be of profound concern for Christians faced with the all-pervasive dominance of state schools, state-subservient churches, state welfare, state media, state planned economy and state medicine. It forms the creeping basis of a *totalitarian society* and an increasingly absolutist one. The cultural crisis facing believers in recent years has unmasked the extent of our technocratic bureaucratization of life and the disturbing totalitarian drift of a complacent society under the sway of a passive, dependent and docile spirit, ready to run to the state for salvation, safety and provision. Yet there is only one true source of provision and salvation for man and His name is Jesus Christ the Lord. The ever-expanding government of peace is upon His shoulders (Is. 9:6-7) and His dominion is an everlasting dominion (Dan. 4: 34-35).

There is then only one truly Christian view of government and politics that is consistent with the gospel of the kingdom and it involves believers in a critical struggle again in our era. As Evan Runner insightfully articulated it:

> The Christian political task involves calling a halt to the expansionist (totalitarian) politics that emerge in the life of the state where men who do not live by the light of the Word of God and having lost almost all sense of *sphere sovereignty* find themselves with a levelled view of the state and society that knows no limits ordained from above, but only more or less arbitrary limits put by the popular will or the ruler. Here is a problem in the modern world which is overcome by the *Christian religion*. In the modern political mind, who is there to call the state to order? The meaning of the office in human life has largely been lost; everyman carries the ultimate light around within himself, in his reason, and thus has an equal right with every other to say what the state shall do. Further it has no recognition of divine ordinances. But in the light of scriptural revelation ... who can better call the state to order than the man who knows himself called to order by the high God? Than the man who trembles before the sovereign law-Word of God. *The Christian political task is thus concerned*

with the inner reformation of political life itself as an aspect of the integral renewal of our whole life in obedience to the divine Word of salvation.[75]

Those who claim allegiance to God in an era of apostasy cannot sit on the fence – we need an undivided heart. We will either be faithful office-bearers calling the state to order in light of the Word of God and His creation ordinances or we will submit ourselves to the arbitrary dictates of the autonomous man and his reason, enabling the ancient idolatry of statism to give shape to the future of our children. Is our ultimate allegiance to the Lord Jesus Christ or to the gods of state like Milcom and Baal in the older testament? In his comments on Zephaniah 1, the great nineteenth century English preacher, Charles Spurgeon, points to the divine perspective on those who on the one hand claim to stand with the Most-High God, while at the same time bow down to the state as god:

These people thought they were safe because they were with both parties. They went with the followers of Jehovah and bowed at the same to Milcom. But duplicity is abominable with God, and His soul hates hypocrisy. The idolater who distinctly gives himself to his false god has one sin less than he who brings his polluted and detestable sacrifice into the temple of the Lord, while his heart is with the world and its sins. To hold with the hare and run with the hounds is a coward's policy. In the common matters of daily life, a double-minded man is despised, but in religion he is loathsome to the last degree ... how should divine justice spare the sinner who knows the right, approves it, and professes to follow it, and all the while loves the evil and gives it dominion in his heart?[76]

It is surely time for the church with its prophetic voice, and for all God's people in the public sphere, to remind all power and authority that Jesus Christ is Lord and declare with the Psalmist:

The wicked will return to Sheol—
all the nations that forget God.
For the oppressed will not always be forgotten;
the hope of the afflicted will not perish forever.

Rise up, Lord! Do not let man prevail;
let the nations be judged in Your presence.
Put terror in them, Lord;
let the nations know they are only men. (Psalm 9:17-20)

NOTES

1   Jean-Jacques Rousseau, *The Social Contract,* translated by Maurice Cranston (New York: Penguin Books, 1968), 89.

2   George Bernard Shaw, *The Intelligent Woman's Guide to Socialism and Capitalism* (New York: Brentano's Publishers, 1928), 456.

3   "G.B. Shaw 'Praises' Hitler," *New York Times*, March 22, 1935, 21.

4   Paul Johnson, *Intellectuals: From Marx and Tolstoy to Sartre and Chomsky* (New York: Harper, 2007), 243.

5   Johnson, *Intellectuals*, 244 ff.

6   See Roger Scruton, *Fools, Frauds and Firebrands: Thinkers of the New Left* (London: Bloomsbury, 2015).

7   Thomas Sowell, *Intellectuals and Society* (New York: Basic Books, 2011), 4.

8   For a vividly dramatized depiction of this situation, read or watch the play The History Boys by Alan Bennett.

9   D.F.M. Strauss, 'Scholarly Communication,' *Danie Strauss*, http://daniestrauss.com/before2009/DS%202008%20on%20Scholarly%20Communication.pdf, accessed May 6, 2021.

10 Sowell, *Intellectuals and Society*, 93.

11 James Hannan, *The Genesis of Science: How the Christian Middle Ages Launched the Scientific Revolution* (Washington, DC: Regnery Publishing, 2011).

12 H. Evan Runner, *Point, Counter Point* (St. Catharines, ON: Paideia Press, 2020), 43, 45-46.

13 Runner, *Point, Counter Point*, 36.

14 Sowell, *Intellectuals and Society*, 10.

15 Sowell, *Intellectuals and Society,* 94.

16 Stephen D. King, *When the Money Runs Out: The End of Western Affluence* (New Haven, CT: Yale University Press 2013), 120.

17 Johnson, *Intellectuals*, 342.

18   Sean L. Field, "Holy Women and the Rise of Royal Power in France," *History Today*, Vol 69, Issue 10, October 2019, 57.

19   Abraham Kuyper, *On the Church: Collected Works in Public Theology* (Bellingham, WA: Lexham Press, 2016), 383.

20   Kuyper, *On the Church*, 387.

21   According to Bennie van der Walt, no less than 66 popes in the course of history have referred to Thomas Aquinas' philosophy and authority. Aquinas was declared a Saint by the Roman church in 1323 and his thought remains critical to understanding Roman Catholicism as well as a resurgent scholasticism amongst evangelicals.

22   Kuyper, *On the Church*, 390.

23   Greg L. Bahnsen, *Theonomy in Christian Ethics* (Nacogdoches, TX: Covenant Media Press, 2002), 505

24   Kuyper, *On the Church*, 413.

25   Frank Dikotter, "The Great Dictators," *History Today*, Vol 69, Issue 10, October 2019, 73.

26   Willem Ouweneel, *The World is Christ's: A Critique of Two Kingdoms Theology* (Toronto: Ezra Press, 2017), 252-254.

27   Ouweneel, *The World*, 256.

28   Ouweneel, *The World*, 258.

29   Ouweneel, *The World*, 261.

30   Geerhardus Vos, *The Kingdom of God and the Church*, (New Jersey: P&R, 1972), 87.

31   Vos, *The Kingdom of God and the Church*, 87.

32   Vos, *The Kingdom of God and the Church*, 77.

33   Herman N. Ridderbos, *The Coming of the Kingdom* (New Jersey: P&R, 1962), 343.

34   Ridderbos, *The Coming*, 354-355.

35   Ridderbos, *The Coming*, 355.

36 Vos, *The Kingdom of God*, 87-88.

37 Vos, *The Kingdom of God*, 88.

38 D.F.M. Strauss, *"Sphere Sovereignty, Solidarity and Subsidiarity," Danie Strauss*, http://daniestrauss.com/selection/DS%202013%20on%20Sphere%20sovereignty,%20solidarity%20and%20subsidiarity.pdf, accessed October 2019, 99-100.

39 Herman Dooyeweerd, *The Christian Idea of the State* (New Jersey: The Craig Press, 1968), 12.

40 Strauss, *Sphere Sovereignty*, 114.

41 K. L. Grasso, "Dignitatis Humanae," in Weigel & Royal, *A Century of Catholic Social Thought, Essays on Rerum Novarum and Nine Other Key Documents* (Lanham: University Press of America, 1991), 95-113.

42 Jan Dengerink, *The Idea of Justice in Christian Perspective* (Oshawa: Wedge Publishing, 1978), 3-4.

43 Dengerink, *The Idea of Justice*, 6.

44 "The NHS is the world's fifth largest employer," *Nuffield Trust*, last modified October 27, 2017, https://www.nuffieldtrust.org.uk/chart/the-nhs-is-the-world-s-fifth-largest-employer.

45 See Robert Louis Wilken, *Liberty in the Things of God: The Christian Origins of Religious Freedom* (New Haven: Yale University Press, 2019), 99-117.

46 Abraham Kuyper, *Christianity as a Life-System: The Witness of a World-View* (Memphis, TN: Christian Studies Centre, 1980), 27.

47 James M. Willson, *The Establishment and Limits of Civil Government: An Exposition of Romans 13:1-7* (Powder Springs, Georgia: American Vision Press, 2009), 14-15.

48 Willson, *The Establishment*, 26.

49 Willson, *The Establishment*, 31. Willson's exegetical argument, which cannot be explored here, is worth reading in full.

50   Kuyper, *Christianity as a Life-System*, 28.

51   Kuyper, *Christianity as a Life-System*, 28.

52   Dooyeweerd, *The Christian Idea of the State*, 11.

53   John Witte, Jr. *Introduction* to Herman Dooyeweerd, *A Christian Theory of Social Institutions* (La Jolla, CA: Herman Dooyeweerd Foundation: 1986), 16-17.

54   Dooyeweerd, *A Christian Theory of Social Institutions*, 17.

55   Kuyper, *On the Church*, 414.

56   Kuyper, *On the Church*, 415.

57   Dooyeweerd, *A Christian Theory of Social Institutions*, 37-38.

58   Dooyeweerd, *A Christian Theory of Social Institutions*, 47.

59   Dooyeweerd, *A Christian Theory of Social Institutions*, 48.

60   Herman Dooyeweerd, *Time, Law and History: Selected Essays, Collected Works*, Series B – Vol. 14, ed. D.F.M. Strauss (Grand Rapids: Paideia Press), 346.

61   Dooyeweerd, *Time, Law and History*, 345-346.

62   Dooyeweerd, *Time, Law and History*, 348.

63   Kuyper, *Christianity as a Life-System*, 35-36.

64   Kuyper, *Christianity as a Life-System*, 35.

65   Danie F.M. Strauss, *Sphere Sovereignty*, (Ezra Institute, March 2019).

66   Kuyper, *On the Church*, 415.

67   Kuyper, *Christianity as a Life System*, 38.

68   Willem Ouweneel, *Power in Service: An Introduction to Christian Political Thought* (St. Catharines: Paideia Press, 2014), 34, 38.

69   Dengerink, *The Idea of Justice*, 26.

70   Dengerink, *The Idea of Justice*, 45.

71   Dooyeweerd, *The Christian Idea of the State*, 10.

72   Jonathan Chaplin, *Herman Dooyeweerd, Christian Philosopher of State and Civil Society* (Indiana: Notre Dame, 2011), 250.

73 Kuyper, *On the Church*, 417.

74 Dooyeweerd, *The Christian Idea of the State*, 11.

75 H. Evan Runner, *Walking in the Way of the Word: The Collected Writings of H. Evan Runner* (St. Catharines: Paideia Press, 2009), 204-205.

76 Charles Haddon Spurgeon, *Morning and Evening* (Wheaton: Crossway Books, 2003), daily reader, November 14.